"This new book by Shawn Perich, a lifetime resident of Lake Superior's coast, takes the mystery out of the North Shore, while adding to the area's appeal. *The North Shore* is a treasure-trove of information ranging from the practical . . . to the historical . . . to the humorous . . . "

The Minnesota Volunteer

"North Shore visitors and locals alike will find that Shawn Perich's book is a valuable in-depth guide for what to do and see along the North Shore. The book fills the gaps between historical documentation and touristy puffery. For sixty-two years I have called the North Shore my home and thought I knew it all—until I read Shawn's book. I rediscovered a lot I knew and discovered a lot I didn't know."

Howard Sivertson, author and painter

"The North Shore assists with a behind-the-scenes exploration, pointing the way away from the crowds and into the quiet, wild majesty that makes the North Shore special."

Duluth News-Tribune

"Perich presents highlights of the North Shore's rich lore—trapping, logging, commercial fishing, shipping. But his obvious loves are the water and the woods . . . After reading the book, anglers will see the North Shore waters in a new light."

Outdoor News

THE NORTH SHORE

A Four-Season Guide
To Minnesota's Favorite Destination

Shawn Perich

Illustrations by David Minix

Pfeifer-Hamilton

Pfeifer-Hamilton Publishers
210 West Michigan
Duluth MN 55802-1908   218-727-0500

The North Shore
A Four-Season Guide to Minnesota's Favorite Destination

Printed in the United States of America by Edwards Brothers Incorporated
10 9 8 7 6 5 4 3 2

Editorial Director: Susan Gustafson
Assistant Editor: Patrick Gross
Art Director: Joy Morgan Dey

Cover photo: Jay Steinke

Library of Congress Cataloging in Publication Data
92-70990

ISBN 0-938586-67-X

To Vikki

Behind every fisherman is a patient woman,
but behind every writer is a saint.

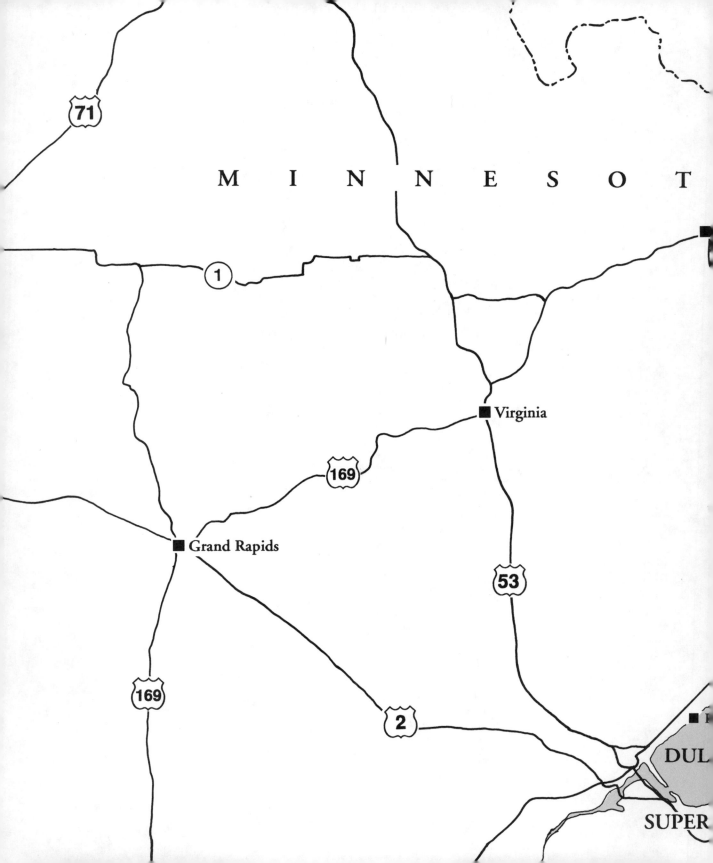

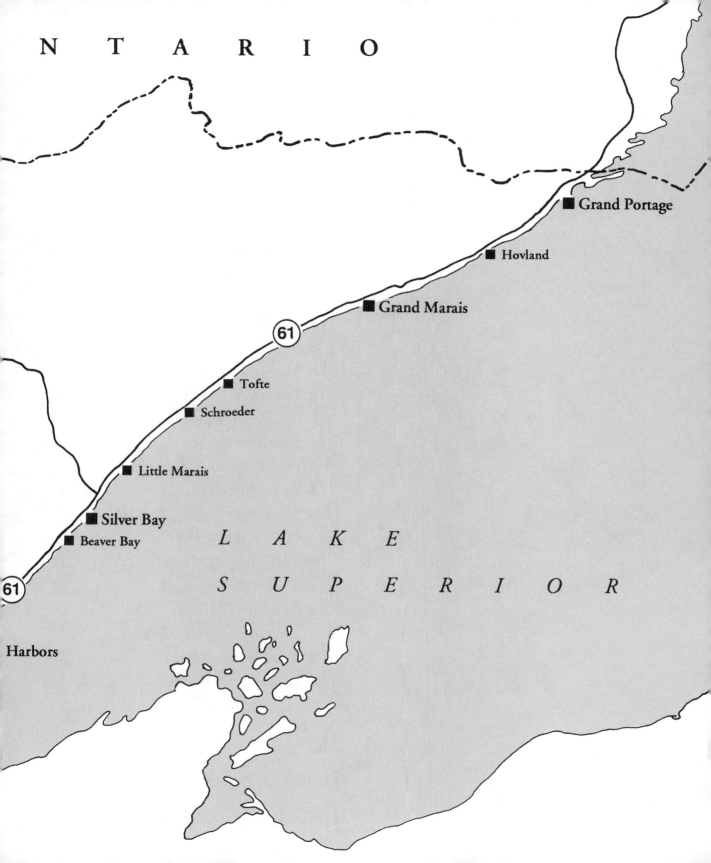

The Old Highway

Lester River to Two Harbors

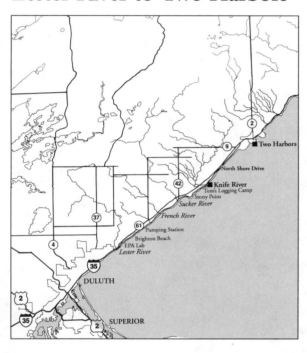

Twists, Turns, and Waterfalls

Two Harbors to Highway 1

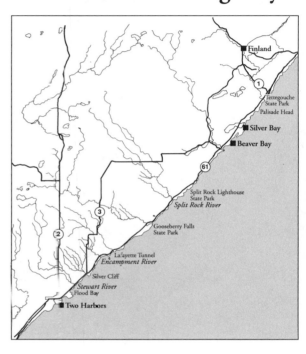

Ski Country

Highway 1 to Cascade

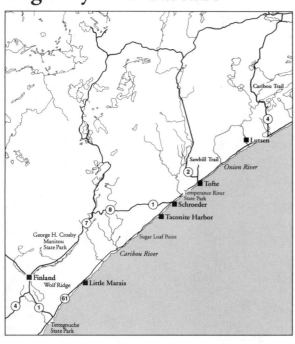

Voyageurs and Fishermen
Cascade to Grand Marais

The Wild Coast

Grand Marais to the Canadian Border

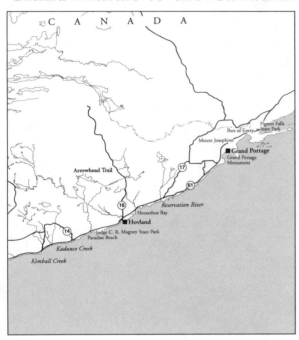

Introduction

My earliest memory of the North Shore is of running along a gravel spit at the mouth of the Split Rock River while waves higher than my head crashed onto the beach. It was June, and my father cast for steelhead while my mother cooked hot dogs over a tiny fire for a picnic lunch. Living in Duluth, we often drove up the Shore when I was a child—fishing, hiking, and picnicking. Trout fishing is in my blood (my father took my mother into the alder jungles of the upper Sucker River a week before I was born), and I began wandering Highway 61 as soon as I could drive.

Like many Duluthians, after college I moved to the Twin Cities to find work. Still, the North Shore beckoned. Weekends and vacations were spent along Highway 61. I remember driving into Minneapolis late one Sunday night, thinking, *if I don't watch it, I'll flip out on this city life and move to the woods before I'm thirty.* I was twenty-eight when I moved to Grand Marais.

Writing this book has given me an opportunity to continue that wandering, to see new sights and meet new people. Many people shared their expertise with me, and this volume would be slim indeed without their help. Some, like Maurice Fiegal at Thomsonite Beach, will always be special to me. Maurice, seventy-six, spent an entire morning telling me about his life's work, collecting thomsonite and turning it into fine jewelery. It wasn't easy for him, because he suffers from an advanced case of Parkinson's disease. Yet his love for thomsonite and the North Shore kept him going through the lengthy interview and a tour of his lapidary shop.

Of course, much of the North Shore's past has previously been carefully researched and documented. I relied upon the work of the Lake County and Cook County historical societies for much of the historical information in this book. Men like Ed Maki, Jr., and Bill Raff have done an excellent job of recording life in the early years. A rainy day spent exploring the public libraries in Silver Bay and Grand Marais will reward you, as it did me, with a wealth of fascinating local material.

As you study North Shore history, you become aware that it has always been the natural resources that have attracted outsiders. First it was fur, then it was minerals, lumber, and fish. Inevitably, the seemingly inexhaustible resources played out. You can't help but wonder if history will repeat itself. Today the resource that brings people to the Shore is its wild beauty, a precious commodity in an increasingly civilized world. Yet in our rush to be here, to savor this wonderful place, we are taming the wild essence that makes the North Shore unique. With new tunnels and highway improvements, the Shore is becoming more easily accessible. Lakeshore homesteads have been sold and subdivided to build summer homes. Resort complexes have sprung up to meet the growing demand for accomodations. You can now drive the family car down forest roads where ten years ago four-wheel-drives feared to tread. How many years will it be before we look back in sadness at the wild beauty we once had?

If nothing else, I hope this book deepens your appreciation for the North Shore, so that you treat this natural wonder with respect. This book covers some, but by no means all, of the places to see and things to do along the Shore. Plenty of discoveries remain for you, and that's really what the North Shore is all about. So, get out and discover your own special places.

Acknowledgments

Contributions of knowledge and expertise by the following persons made this book possible: Beth Alpert, John Amren, Rick Anderson, John Bachar, Scott Beattie, Tom Biele, Bill and Beth Blank, Loretta Bloomquist, Sandy Bugge, Sam Cook, Bob Drummond, Terry Eggum, Kim Ekert, Maurice and Tania Feigal, Al Hodapp, Mike Larson, Pete Lenski, Phil Leverfedge, Tom Ludwig, Orvis and Sandy Lunke, BJ Smith Kohlstedt, Mark Kovacovich, Bill Majewski, Chuck Mattson, Jeff McMorrow, Ron Nickerson, Diane Pelto, Bill Peterson, Tom Peterson, Roland Quinn, Lee Radzak, Lauren Richter, Mary Somnis, Becky Spears, Mark Spinler, Paul Sunberg, Don Van Nispen, Jim Vick, and Holly Young.

Decisions, decisions. Two Harbors in twenty minutes? Or follow the shoreline and enjoy the view? The expressway offers convenience but sacrifices the view. It takes a little longer to get there on the old highway, but you follow the shoreline most of the way. Time is on your side when you vacation, so we're taking the scenic route. If you're in a hurry, skip ahead to the chapter on Two Harbors. We'll catch up with you.

Allow some time to enjoy the lake along this stretch. In fact, why not buy some smoked fish and enjoy an impromptu picnic at Brighton Beach or Stony Point? If you've brought a bike, the old highway is perfect for pedaling. Runners like it, too, and thousands come every June to run Grandma's Marathon from Two Harbors to Duluth. This is the most civilized portion of the North Shore Drive, a suburban extension of Duluth. Nevertheless, you'll find a number of quaint and quiet resorts along the way.

Two Harbors

North Shore Drive

Knife River
Tom's Logging Camp
Stony Point
Sucker River

French River

Pumping Station
Brighton Beach
EPA Lab
Lester River

DULUTH

The Old Highway
Lester River to Two Harbors

SUPERIOR

Compass Points

Directions given by a Duluthian or North Shore local can be confusing. They don't seem to know north from east or south from west. The sign may read North Highway 61, but if your car is pointed toward Canada a local will say you're heading east. If the auto is aimed at Duluth they'll say you're going west.

You can clear up the confusion by looking carefully at a North Shore map. Even though you're headed "up north," Highway 61 goes more east than north. Inland routes such as Highway 1 and the Gunflint Trail go northward.

In this book Highway 61 directions are referred to as east and west. Therefore Two Harbors is east of Duluth and Lutsen is west of Grand Marais. Confused? Don't be. Just remember that if you turn south you'll get very wet.

Lester River

MILEPOST 4 According to the Minnesota Department of Transportation, the North Shore begins at Twelfth Avenue East in Duluth—the starting point for State Highway 61. However, not until you cross the Lester River Bridge do you first see the lake up close and leave the city behind. For most of us, this marks the real beginning of the North Shore Drive.

In their hurry to get farther up the highway, many travelers cross Lester River without slowing down. That's unfortunate, because this river is one of Duluth's many wild treasures. In recent years, the city has taken some of the wildness out of the lower river by installing walks, overlooks, and stairways, but there is still beauty in this urban setting.

A stately white building on the west bank at the mouth of the river was the first federal fish hatchery built on Lake Superior. Water was piped in from the east side of the river where you can still see reservoir ponds. The hatchery closed shortly after the turn of the century, and the University of Minnesota, Duluth, now owns the building.

About one block upriver from the Highway 61 bridge is a large pool called the Japp Hole. In the spring and fall anglers line its banks, looking for the trout and salmon that enter the river when the water is high. The Lester offers good fishing if you don't mind crowds. Solitary types would be better off trying their luck in rivers farther up the shore.

Just above the Superior Street bridge the river divides. The west fork is Amity Creek. Occidental Boulevard, the Seven Bridges Road, follows Amity's serpentine course up the pine-clad hillside, eventually connecting with the easternmost portion of Skyline Drive near Hawk Ridge. The stone bridges date back to the Depression-era WPA public works projects. Keep a sharp eye for kids who look wet—Amity has locally famous swimming holes. During the winter you can go tobogganing—at your own risk—on the slopes of the now-closed Lakeview Ski Area.

At Skyline Parkway a gated gravel road continues up the creek. Hikers and mountain bikers will find that it leads to a quick escape from civilization. The road intersects with the North Shore Corridor Trail. Skyline Parkway, which is gravel here, leads west to the overlook at Hawk Ridge. In autumn birds of prey numbering in the hundreds of thousands funnel past here on their southward migration. The birds circle far overhead in huge flocks called kettles. Birders from across the country come to see this spectacular natural event. Binoculars are a must.

If you follow the road up the east side of the river, you'll find a small parking area about two blocks above the Superior Street intersection. A short path leads to a stunning waterfall, an unsung gem. The path connects into the network of hiking trails in Duluth's Lester Park. During the winter, the city maintains a groomed ski trail system throughout this area. City-owned Lester Park Golf Course, across the road, recently has been expanded to twenty-seven holes.

Just past the river, the first information booth along Highway 61 offers information about accommodations and attractions along the length of the shore. The venerable North Shore Association operates it from May to October.

Spring Lunacy

Rainbow smelt are relative newcomers to the Great Lakes. Native to the Atlantic Ocean, smelt were first introduced to the Great Lakes system via Michigan waters before World War I.

Originally it was thought that the small, silvery fish would provide a food source for larger species. As it turned out, smelt nearly destroyed an important native fish, the lake herring. Voracious smelt preyed upon newly hatched herring. Their appetites, coupled with other human-caused environmental changes, led to the virtual collapse of the North Shore's commercial fishing industry.

During the 1950s and 1960s, when the bottom fell out of native fish populations such as lake trout, herring, and whitefish, the smelt population exploded. The fish then rose to its own strange prominence. Two generations of Midwesterners often had their first North Shore experience on a drunken, half-remembered smelting trip.

Smelt spawn in the spring when the rivers run high with snowmelt, usually a couple of weeks before Minnesota's general fishing opener. This is a restless, edgy time for Midwesterners. Winter has finally broken. The weather is nice, but there isn't much to do. Perhaps that's why smelting became a bacchanalian spring rite.

Maybe it was because smelt run best on warm spring nights. Sometimes there wouldn't be much activity until the early morning hours. If you weren't out there waiting, you'd miss it. Part of it could have been that hitting it big during this piscatorial orgy produced emotions similar to those felt by the pioneers when they first saw the buffalo—the supply seemed inexhaustible.

So when the smelt came, people loaded up. At the peak of the run, which lasted anywhere from a couple of nights to a week or more, the stream bottom from one bank to the other would be black with smelt. You could scoop them up with your hands. Instead people used dip nets, filling everything from plastic ice cream pails to garbage cans. If you stumbled and spilled the load while climbing a steep hill back to the parking lot, big deal. There were no limits, so you could always go back and get more.

The morning after a big run the banks would be littered with dead smelt, far more than the seagulls could possibly eat. It was a good idea to stay upwind of the largest piles.

Smelt fries sponsored by churches, VFWs, and other community groups became spring institutions from Duluth to Des Moines. Deep-fried in batter they were tasty, provided you ate them but once or twice a year.

Smelting was always an activity of paradoxes. How else could you earn brownie points with the minister by gathering the main ingredient for a fund-raising dinner and get falling-down drunk at the same time? What other fish could you eat bones-and-all and not worry about choking? Where else could you go fishing with a net and not get arrested?

However, not even hordes of dip-netters could keep smelt in check. During the summer large numbers of dead smelt floated up on the beach. Apparently, there were just too many of them.

Changes occurred in Lake Superior fish populations during the 1970s and 1980s. Trout and salmon stocking increased, so more of these large predators swam in the lake. Herring, especially in the western end of the lake, staged a comeback. Smelt numbers dwindled.

Today smelt runs are but a fraction of what they were just a few years ago, when it was estimated the annual run yielded 750,000 pounds of fish. A few smelters still make the journey up the Shore, but most dip-netters are locals looking for a few meals and some fish bait.

It appears that the natural balance is being restored to Lake Superior's fishery.

Smelting tips

Smelt run up the rivers to spawn when the water temperature reaches forty-two degrees. They gather offshore in schools and then move into shoreline shallows and tributary streams around sundown. They are not powerful swimmers, so look for them near the river mouth. Rarely do they ascend rapids.

Timing the run is more tricky in this era of few smelt. Radio stations and newspapers often post updates. A general rule to remember is that the further from the source, the less reliable the information. A long-distance call to a tourist information center, motel, bait shop, or gas station in the North Shore community you plan to visit is an inexpensive way to get accurate information.

Two of the more popular smelting rivers are the Lester and the Knife. Several streams are now closed to smelting, including Sucker River, Little Sucker River, Silver Creek, Crow Creek, Encampment River, and French River. A fishing license is required.

Travel Time

The North Shore Drive isn't a freeway. At best, it's a winding two-lane highway fraught with hazards such as deer and tractor-trailers. On summer days you can add such driving challenges as motorhomes, bikes, sight-seers, and congested areas. It's hard to estimate how long it will take you to drive from point A to point B.

Generally speaking, you'll average fifty miles an hour, but on holiday weekends and other busy times you won't go that fast. If making time is important to you, travel early in the morning.

The speed limit on the Shore is fifty-five miles per hour and there are numerous reduced speed zones. Obeying the speed limit will help you avoid accidents as well as tickets. Remember, you're here to enjoy yourself, not to set a new land speed record.

White-tailed deer are the most common hazard encoun-
tered by motorists. They are commonly seen in the morning
and evening, but may leap out in front of you at any time of
day. During the winter and spring you'll see dozens of them.
On some stretches, especially beyond Grand Marais, moose
are common. Because they are so dark, moose are especially
difficult to see at night.

Always slow down for the state parks and for communities. People frequently cross the highway in these areas—
sometimes without looking for traffic. Children may dart
out from anywhere.

On occasion you will end up behind a long line of traffic
following a slow-moving motorhome or other vehicle. Be
sure you can see far enough ahead before you pass. You'll
encounter two passing lanes between Silver Creek Cliff and
Gooseberry Falls.

Highway 61 is especially dangerous during foggy or
snowy weather. Slight changes in elevation affect the air
temperature, so you may encounter snow in some areas and
sleet in others. State highway crews do an excellent job of
keeping the roadway clear, but sometimes the snow accumu-
lates so quickly they can't keep up. Take it easy. It's better to
arrive late than to go into the ditch.

Environmental Research Laboratory

MILEPOST 4 Just east of Lester River is a research and development facility for studying freshwater pollution.
Opened in 1967, the laboratory has been under the
U.S. Environmental Protection Agency's (EPA) wing
since the agency was formed in 1970. The lab's scientists
determine what concentrations of pesticides, toxic substances,
and hazardous wastes are safe for freshwater plants and
animals.

The laboratory has "wet" testing facilities, which allow it
to run up to fifty aquatic tests at one time. Instruments at
the lab can measure chemicals that occur in a few parts per

billion. (Lab officials say that one part per billion is the equivalent of one ounce of chocolate syrup in 7.8 million gallons of milk.)

Much of the research is done on fathead minnows, a popular bait minnow which fishermen call chubs. Scientists use the minnows, a representative species, to study how pollutants move through, react with, and affect the life processes of an aquatic environment.

The results of research conducted at this lab have nationwide implications. Experimental data have been used for the enforcement of environmental law in cases involving DDT, PCBs, and mining wastes. Studies of chemicals in fish have led to the discovery of pollution sources.

The laboratory is currently involved in the study of exotic species (creatures that are not native to Lake Superior's waters) such as the zebra mussel. It is also examining the impact of global climate change on the aquatic environment.

The lab is not open for public tours.

Brighton Beach

MILEPOST 5 No, this isn't the place Neil Simon wrote about. This Brighton Beach is an undeveloped rocky coast that was recently considered as a site for a state boat launch and harbor. Concerned citizens voiced heartfelt opposition to the plan, fearful that the breakwalls and boating traffic would disrupt the serenity and beauty of Brighton Beach. Boating boosters were soon looking for another site.

The cutoff for the Brighton Beach Road, just past the tourist information booth, loops back to the old highway. You'll find plenty of parking and excellent access to the lakeshore. The offshore area is popular with anglers, so from shore you can watch sport fishing boats, as well as sailboats and larger ships.

LESTER RIVER TO TWO HARBORS

The immensity of Lake Superior is overwhelming. As you stand on its shore before you lies one-tenth of the world's fresh water—three quadrillion gallons. Superior holds as much water as the rest of the Great Lakes combined—enough to flood North and South America with water a foot deep. The lake is 350 miles long and 160 miles wide. Its maximum depth is 1,333 feet.

When the last glacier melted, Lake Superior was even larger. A keen eye can still see the former shore of Glacial Lake Duluth along Duluth's Skyline Drive—500 feet above the lake—as well as in other locations. At that time the lake flowed into the Mississippi River via the channel of today's Bois Brule and St. Croix rivers in Wisconsin. The present outlet is the St. Mary's River at Sault St. Marie, Michigan.

First-time visitors are often struck by the lake's clarity. You can easily see the bottom in thirty feet of water. Divers can see over fifty feet. Superior is the cleanest of the Great Lakes, and most of its fish are safe to eat. An exception are very large lake trout, which, during their long lives, have accumulated pollutants in their body fat, should be eaten in only limited amounts. Major sources of pollution are large cities and a handful of industrial sites—primarily paper mills—around the lake.

Superior's size and cold temperature—its water averages forty degrees—influence local weather. In the summer it is often chilly near the lakeshore and warm just a few miles inland, but winter temperatures are significantly warmer near the lake.

The lake is famed for its fierce storms, the worst usually occurring during November and March. Storm waves are oceanlike, reaching heights of ten to twenty feet. Occasionally during storms you can see waves rolling over the piers at the Duluth ship canal. Over the years those storms have sunk about 350 ships.

The St. Lawrence Seaway connects Lake Superior with

The Greatest Lake

the Atlantic Ocean via the lower Great Lakes. More than one thousand ships, ranging from Great Lakes ore carriers to oceangoing freighters, visit the Duluth-Superior harbor annually. The "salties" take on grain destined for overseas, while the lake carriers haul coal and taconite. The best places to see the ships are near Duluth, Silver Bay, and Taconite Harbor; in other places, the boats are often far offshore.

Is Baikal bigger?

Russia's Lake Baikal has nearly double Lake Superior's water volume, but less than half its surface area. Baikal contains 5,518 cubic miles of water compared to Superior's 2,934. However, Lake Superior's surface area covers 31,700 square miles, while Baikal covers only 12,500. Lake Baikal is 397 miles long and 55 miles wide. Baikal is over a mile deep; its maximum depth is 5,313 feet. The surface of the lake is 1,360 feet above sea level and it is 25 million years old.

Lakewood Water Treatment Plant

MILEPOST 7 Duluth and some neighboring communities draw their water supply from Lake Superior via the Lakewood pumping station.

The building along the shoreline, with its interesting turret, was built during the 1890s, following a typhoid epidemic thought to be caused by lake water drawn from a polluted downtown site. Duluthians drank untreated water from Lakewood until a second typhoid outbreak occurred in the early 1900s. Then the city began adding chlorine to the water. Fluoridation, required by Minnesota statute, began in 1968.

The treatment facility north of the highway was built in 1976, in response to the Reserve Mining controversy. Taconite tailings dumped into the lake by the company contained cancer-causing asbestos particles. The treatment facility filters suspended particles, including asbestos, from the water. The amount of asbestos in the water began declining when the company started onland disposal of taconite tailings at Milepost 7.

The water treatment plant intake line has a diameter of five feet and extends fifteen hundred feet into the lake, drawing water from a depth of seventy-five feet. The facility pumps about twenty-one million gallons per day, including five million gallons for Lake Superior Paper Industries in Duluth. The facility's maximum pumping capacity is about thirty-two million gallons per day. Anticipating future water demands, the city plans to increase its capacity.

If you'd like to inspect the station's century-old architecture, you can park in a small lot east of the station. The shoreline in front of the facility is popular with shorecasters. Make sure you crank your lures in quickly, because the area is shallow and rocky.

Mussel no match for cold lake

Elsewhere in the Great Lakes the zebra mussel—a tiny European clam that hitchhiked across the Atlantic in ship ballasts—has proliferated in colonies that clog water intake lines and cause expensive damage. Experts don't anticipate a similar problem at the Lakewood pumping station because Lake Superior water is just too darn cold. Zebra mussels need fifty-five-degree water in order to reproduce. Off Lakewood the water temperature averages an icy forty-three degrees. However, the mussels have been found in the warmer waters of the Duluth-Superior harbor. Industrial facilities located on the harbor could have future problems with the troublesome little clam.

June vacationers are a breed apart. They might be anglers, or fog freaks, or they might be marathon runners. June can be a dreary month on the Shore. The sun disappears for days on end when the fog rolls in. The temperature is springlike, even though it's summer everywhere else. In some years ice

Grandma's Marathon

still lies along the shoreline and many people still wear warm jackets..

But every June more than 5,000 runners make the 26.2-mile run from Two Harbors to Duluth. Many say the cool temperatures make for better running. Maybe that's why Grandma's has become America's eighth-largest marathon, attracting runners from around the world. In the first year, 1977, the race had 150 entrants; in 1985 it had more than 8,000. The marathon follows the Scenic North Shore Drive. Race watchers should get an early start. It is often difficult to find parking near the course, especially in Duluth.

Perfect for Picnics

Duluth maintains several waysides along the scenic highway beyond Brighton Beach. Although the McQuade Road near Talmadge River marks the city limit, city land extends eastward along the shoreline all the way to Stony Point. During the 1920s Duluth businessman Chester Congdon gave the lakeshore property to the city as a gift. When Congdon learned of plans to build a highway along the lakeshore, he instructed his real estate agents to purchase available shoreline land, as well as property bordering the small Duluth trout stream that now bears his name. The land was given with the stipulation that what wasn't used as highway right-of-way would forever remain parkland. The waysides aren't fancy, just a few parking spots and a picnic table or two, but few would ask for more.

The waysides provide access to the lakeshore, although in some places you have to clamber down a clay bank to reach the water. Shoreline erosion is a problem along here and sometimes eroded soil clouds the near-shore waters.

Between Talmadge and Sucker River lies Bluebird Landing. You can launch a cartop craft or a *very* small trailered boat there, but the launch site is crude, to say the least. Parking is extremely limited. Waves and ice are wearing away the remains of an ancient cement dock left from a former fishing operation. You can splash through ankle-deep water between the dock and shore and clamber up on the concrete to shore-cast.

| MILEPOST |
| 11 |

French River is a fishy place. Below the highway anglers line up along the lakeshore to try for trout and salmon. Above the highway, at the French River Hatchery, the Minnesota Department of Natural Resources (DNR) produces trout and salmon for stocking. A walking path leads you through the facility.

The Minnesota DNR has only one cold-water hatchery on the North Shore because, surprisingly, of a lack of adequate water supplies. Young trout and salmon need water with a consistent temperature in the forties and fifties. Lake Superior's temperature hovers in the frigid thirties for much of the year. Stream water varies from near freezing in the winter to the seventies or higher in the summer.

At other hatcheries, spring water (a limited commodity on the North Shore) provides cold water at a constant temperature. At French River, water taken from Lake Superior is heated to the proper temperature. Recycled several times through a bio-filtering process, which removes fish wastes, the water returns to the lake as clean as it came out.

Many of the fish raised at the hatchery originate from the eggs of fish trapped in a weir on the French River, a short distance above the highway. Trout and salmon swimming upstream to spawn are captured there. When the fish "ripen," workers strip eggs from the female and milt from the males. If you walk quietly along the riverbank and look into the water, you'll often see large trout or salmon. No fishing is allowed in this portion of the French River.

The French River Hatchery produces rainbow trout, lake trout, chinook salmon, brook trout, splake, herring, and walleye.

Regardless of the weather or season, you'll usually see a

French River

few anglers casting into Lake Superior from the French River shoreline. Because a variety of trout and salmon species are stocked here, usually a fish or two lurks offshore. In fact, French River may be the most consistent shore-fishing location on the Minnesota coast. And don't think you'll be fishing for toy-sized stocked trout; the average trout or salmon caught here is measured in pounds rather than inches.

The species of fish you are most likely to catch varies with the season. During winter and spring chunky Kamloops rainbow trout are the stars of the show. Anglers both cast and fish through the ice for them—occasionally on the same day. Ice conditions on Lake Superior vary with the wind, so play it safe and stay close to shore.

In late spring and early summer you may catch steelhead, lake trout, Kamloops, coho salmon, Atlantic salmon, or chinook salmon. Chinooks take center stage in late summer, when they begin congregating near the river in preparation for their fall spawning run.

How do you catch them?

French River fishing veterans often snicker at the angling efforts of visitors. You may be an accomplished angler back home, but Lake Superior quickly humbles those new to its waters. If you are a novice to Lake Superior fishing, seek out local advice. A few minutes talking with local anglers will get you started in the right direction. However, don't expect them to tell you *everything*. North Shore fishing savvy is hard-earned, and few successful anglers are willing to give out their trade secrets.

The regulars often use specialized tackle, but the average spinning rig will suffice. Use light line; six-pound test is adequate for most situations. Make sure you set the drag on your reel so the fish can take line when they run.

Stop at a local tackle shop and ask what techniques are currently catching fish, because methods vary through the seasons. Find out which lures and baits are productive. Shore anglers often cast with spoons and spinners. Sometimes they still-fish with spawn sacks, nightcrawlers, wigglers, or dead smelt. Experience teaches the special tricks for catching each of the many trout and salmon species, but a casual angler, casting a Rapala, Little Cleo, Krocodile, or Roostertail, stands a chance of catching something.

Be sure to read the state fishing regulations before you fish. You must have a state trout stamp to fish Lake Superior and its tributaries. When fishing the lower reaches of North Shore streams, you cannot use treble hooks—even on lures. Although you may actually see large salmon or trout swimming in the rivers, don't try to snag them or catch them by hand—both methods are illegal.

If you are serious about catching a fish from Lake Superior, get out at dawn. Trout and salmon are sensitive to light and are most likely to be near shore during the early morning hours. Pick a fishing spot near a river mouth, off a breakwall, or along a rocky point. Even if you don't catch anything—a frequent occurrence on the North Shore— watching the sunrise over Lake Superior will reward you for getting up early.

Sucker River

MILEPOST 13 A chunk of concrete left from a long-forgotten logging dock marks the mouth of the Sucker River. The name Sucker was given by the Indians, and the river still receives a run of these bugle-mouthed fish every spring. But the spring and fall runs of trout and salmon overshadow the sucker run.

Anglers haunt the stretch of river between the expressway and the scenic highway. It tumbles over several waterfalls, which lakerun fish can ascend. If you look into the concrete culvert beneath the expressway, you can see water baffles, which were installed to make it easier for the fish to swim upstream.

Whether or not you enjoy fishing, the shaded pathways following the river make for pleasant strolling. Watch out for muddy areas, especially in the spring or after rains.

Stony Point

MILEPOST 15

Stony Pont is exactly that: a rocky ledge jutting into the lake. Across the highway from Tom's Logging Camp you'll find a road which follows the lakeshore. The road reaches the lake west of the point, where erosion has damaged an overlook situated on a clay bank above the lake. Continue along the road and you'll pass some fishing shacks and then come to a stretch of ledge rock beach. Pull over and take a walk.

On warm, summer days Stony Point becomes what Duluthians call crowded, which means you don't have the beach to yourself. The beach is popular with picnicers and shorecasters. In fact, so many casting spoons are lost on the underwater ledges that scuba divers come here to collect them—often to sell them back to the anglers who lost them in the first place!

Stony Point is an excellent place to watch or photograph the waves when the lake is rough. Deep water rollers crash against the rocks, tossing spray far into the air. Keep your distance from the water's edge, because an errant wave could pluck you from the rocks.

When the wind and waves are high, be sure to watch the gulls. They seem to enjoy Superior's stormy days. Often you'll see them soaring just above the angry breakers. They'll even land and ride the swells, bobbing up and down like so many unconcerned corks.

Just east of the point is a small gravel beach where you might find agates. If you don't, try looking in the gravel along the road. The road, by the way, loops back out to the old highway.

It's a sad fact that you can rarely swim in Lake Superior. Even in midsummer the water is heart-stoppingly cold. If you fell overboard from a boat, you could die of hypothermia on a sweltering August day. Only during a prolonged stretch of hot, calm weather do the near-shore waters warm enough to let you take a dip. Even then the water will likely be on the chilly side.

So in the big lake, divers have all the fun. A good wet suit will let you stay in the water for up to a half hour, even in the winter when water temperatures hover just above freezing. Despite the cold, Lake Superior is relatively safe for divers, because it has no treacherous currents. You can see fifty feet or more in the clear waters.

If you don't have a boat, you can dive from shore in a number of different places. The old city docks at Fourth Avenue East in Duluth are a good place to start. These docks were used before the ship canal, now spanned by the Aerial Lift Bridge, was built. Duluth divers often dive here at night. Because of the proximity to the stained waters of the St. Louis River, visibility is limited, but look carefully along the bottom and you may see artifacts such as snuff jars.

The Lester River and Brighton Beach areas are easily accessible and you can swim to depths of about forty feet. This is a good area for divers to look for agates. Further up the old North Shore Drive are Stony Point and the Buchanan townsite. Waters off the point average about twenty-five feet, while you can reach sixty feet off Buchanan. A wayside and historical marker mark the Buchanan site.

Depths of ninety feet are found at the Two Harbors breakwall. You can swim around the boulders, and you may see trout and other marine life. Offshore is the wreck of the *Ely,* but you need a boat to reach it. River mouths such as the Gooseberry also provide good diving sites, and you may find items that have washed down the river. Some divers have found fur-trade-era artifacts along the North Shore.

Beneath the Surface

Certified divers can rent equipment from at least one Duluth dive shop, and organized weekend dives welcome those new to the lake. Snorkeling is also growing in popularity. Again, though, a wet suit or dry suit is necessary gear.

Tom's Logging Camp

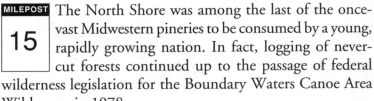

The North Shore was among the last of the once-vast Midwestern pineries to be consumed by a young, rapidly growing nation. In fact, logging of never-cut forests continued up to the passage of federal wilderness legislation for the Boundary Waters Canoe Area Wilderness in 1978.

The early days of logging were one of the most colorful periods in North Shore history. Massive, valuable white pine covered a wild and roadless land. Lumber camps were outposts on the edge of raw wilderness. It took a special breed of men to get those trees from the forest to the sawmill. "In all probability there has never been a more rugged class of men than those that did the logging in the northern forests between 1880 and 1920," reads a sign above one display at Tom's Logging Camp Museum. Certainly they weren't drawn by the lure of big money. Monthly wages were twenty-six dollars for a sawyer, thirty-five dollars for a four-horse teamster, forty dollars for a blacksmith, and sixty dollars for a cook.

The displays of logging equipment at Tom's Logging Camp vividly show the rough life. The early loggers had no chainsaws, skidders, or other gasoline-powered equipment. Humans and horses supplied the power.

The museum replicates the arrangement of a logging camp, with a harness shop, a cook shanty, a bunkhouse, a horse barn, and a warehouse. Each is filled with the tools and equipment it would have housed. The collection of antique logging equipment here is one of the most extensive anywhere.

At Tom's you'll also find a commercial fishing museum

complete with herring skiffs, nets, fish boxes, and old sport tackle. Local anglers contributed most of the fishing collection. Another building contains a Victorian household collection and a potpourri of antiques from bear traps to an electric chair.

The museum charges an admission fee. Of course, not everyone in the family will be enthralled by old harnesses and rusty sawblades. Shoppers can browse in the souvenir shop. Kids will find rabbits wandering the grounds, and penned deer and goats. Anglers who are low on either luck or patience can fish for the hefty rainbows swimming in the trout pond.

Knife River

MILEPOST 18 In April the Knife River runs dirty and swollen. Below the falls, just downstream from the expressway, anglers stand shoulder-to-shoulder in waist-deep icy water, hoping to catch a steelhead from Minnesota's best known steelhead stream. Here, as on few other North Shore rivers, steelhead can jump the falls and swim all the way upstream to the headwaters, so spawning fish have access to about seventy miles of river.

The Knife once drew massive runs of steelhead, but during the 1980s the population declined sharply. Anglers still catch a few of these silvery lakerun rainbow trout, but now they can keep only one and it must be at least twenty-eight inches long. Smaller steelhead must be released unharmed. Biologists hope the catch-and-release program will result in more spawning fish to restore the population.

A number of years ago the Minnesota DNR dynamited pockets into the huge waterfalls below the expressway to give steelhead an easier upstream passage. No fishing is allowed at the falls because migrating fish congregate in the pools. However, you'll find no better place to watch leaping fish. You can see fish from either the east or west bank, although at times one side may be better than the other. Watch places where the water tumbles over the rocks and be patient. Soon you'll see one of these large trout arching from the water. The best fish watching is from mid-April to mid-May.

The community of Knife River has a long history. In 1854, not long after the North Shore was opened to settlement, prospectors discovered veins of copper in the river bottom. However, no one became rich mining Knife River copper. Later, the Alger-Smith company shipped pine logs from here. The remains of the company's dock stand on the west side of the river mouth.

Knife River was also a prominent commercial fishing port. Some netting of herring still takes place in the offshore waters. Knife River shops sell smoked herring, a North Shore treat, along with other smoked fish. You can work off the calories by hiking the trail following the west bank of the river between the old highway and the expressway.

Knife River Marina

MILEPOST 19 The Knife River Marina is the largest North Shore boating facility. Boaters currently have limited access to the waters of Lake Superior, although controversial plans have been proposed to construct other marinas along the Shore. With dockage for about one hundred boats, Knife River is by far the largest marina between Duluth and Thunder Bay. Some local boosters say boating could provide the next big boost to the Shore's tourism economy.

The marina caters to sport anglers, charter captains, sailors, and power boaters. Knife River is a full-service marina offering gas, diesel, and pump-out services. Transient slips are available. For a fee, boaters can launch trailered craft at the marina's ramp.

Visitors are welcome to walk around the grounds and docks as long as they remember some simple rules: stay out of the way (this

is a business) and stay off the boats. Even landlubbers will find the marina interesting. During the summer it is a watery hive of activity. You can watch the comings and goings of a variety of pleasure craft. On the east side of the marina you can walk to the lake for a view of gull-covered Knife Island.

The easiest way to enjoy a day on Lake Superior is by taking a charter fishing trip. However, an enjoyable day on the water begins with planning at home. Here are a few tips:

Consider your group. Is it your family, a few friends, or a group of business associates? Do you want to catch big fish, many fish, or a certain kind of fish, or would you just like to have a pleasant day on the water? Remember, having fun should be your primary objective.

Try to schedule your trip well in advance. The captain may be booked up during the prime fishing months. Charter captains operate in every community from Duluth to Grand Portage. You can find charter captains either by calling the tourist information office in the area you plan to visit or through advertisements in outdoor publications or by word of mouth. A call to a local bait shop or motel will also provide you with some names.

When you contact the captain, don't be afraid to ask questions. A good place to start is by telling him what your objectives are so he knows what you expect and can determine how to best serve you. Although the terms and techniques may be unfamiliar, ask some questions about tackle and equipment. How large is the captain's boat? How many lines can he fish? How well will his craft accommodate your party? Are the fish cleaned by his crew? Is ice provided?

Ask about the minimum charge and the cost per person. Make sure you know whether it is a full- or half-day trip. Rates vary among captains. Some charge more because they've developed reputations as good anglers.

Successful Charter Fishing

Ask what you should bring along. You will probably need food and beverages, sunscreen, and a hat. Regardless of the weather forecast, bring a warm jacket. It's often chilly on Lake Superior. Also, don't forget your camera.

When it comes to fishing Lake Superior, weather can sabotage the best-laid plans. Listen to forecasts. If bad weather is predicted, call the captain before you leave home and ask what he suggests. You may have to postpone your trip.

Although you can generally expect to catch fish, it is possible to get skunked. If fishing has been poor, the captain will often tell you before heading out. If you have a bad day, it's not necessarily the captain's fault. It's his job to lead you to the fish, but sometimes the fish just refuse to cooperate.

If you've enjoyed the trip, it's proper to tip the captain. There are no set rates or percentages, so use your own judgment. If you feel the captain deserves something extra, offer it to him with your thanks.

Two Harbors

MILEPOST 25 You can see little of Two Harbors from Highway 61. If you're in a hurry, the stoplights will irritate you, but if you're hungry, you can find several good places to eat, and if you're curious, take a right at the first lights and spend some time exploring the town.

Two Harbors is a quintessential northern Minnesota community. Timber and steel form its foundations, but today's third- and fourth-generation inhabitants have diversified the extraction-based economy. Still, you'll see plenty of evidence of lumbering and mining.

Pulp trucks rumble in from the hinterlands, and iron-ore carriers bound for steel mills on the lower lakes sidle up to the docks to receive taconite hauled by rail from Iron Range communities. Northern Minnesota provides essential raw materials for the entire nation.

Contrasting with this broad-shouldered image is Two Harbors' newer role as a tourist community. Recreational boaters launch their crafts at the new DNR access against a backdrop of ore docks. Tourists inspect two steam locomotives outside the historical society museum. And some locals wonder just how far to take this "tourism thing."

In recent years the town has made progress in promoting tourism. The downtown area received a facelift. The DNR boat access and parking area made the harbor more attractive to boaters and nonboaters alike. The Lake County Historical Society Museum, the lighthouse, and the new 3M Museum are first-rate attractions. Two Harbors has managed to get on the tourism map without compromising its identity.

Agate Bay on the west and Burlington Bay on the east are the two harbors for which the community is named. Pioneers, attracted by good fishing and plentiful timber, first settled on the shores of Agate Bay during the 1850s, and a sawmill was established at Burlington Bay around the same time. In 1888, the town was renamed Two Harbors and the county seat was moved there from Beaver Bay.

The town grew rapidly after the Merritt brothers discovered iron ore on the Mesabi range. In 1884, Charlemagne Tower left Agate Bay with a steam engine destined for an iron ore mine in Tower, even though the railroad had yet to be completed. In June, he returned with the community's first shipment of ore, ten railroad cars carrying a total of 220 tons. By the 1890s, six docks on Burlington Bay serviced fifteen hundred vessels per year. In 1915, the first steel ore dock (earlier ones were made of wood), Dock #6, was built. Steel that helped win the first and second world wars began as ore shipped through this port.

In the early days the Iron Range produced high-grade soft ore. However, after decades of mining, the high-grade ore was depleted. E. W. Davis, head of the University of Minnesota Mines Experiment Station, worked on development of a process by which steel could be made from taconite, a hard rock containing 25 to 30 percent iron. In

1955 the world's first taconite processing plant opened in Silver Bay. Northern Minnesota has a tremendous supply of taconite, and the process breathed new life into the state's iron mining industry. Today only occasional natural ore shipments are made; taconite is a mainstay for the industry. Most of the taconite shipped from Two Harbors comes from the USX plant in Mountain Iron. The Duluth, Missabe and Iron Range Railroad hauls it to Two Harbors, and the Great Lakes Fleet carries it across the lakes. Both are owned by TransStar of Pennsylvania.

The only months when no ships visit Two Harbors are January, February, and March. A good place to view the shipping activity during the rest of the year is from the breakwall on the east side of Agate Bay. If you're lucky, you may be standing at the end of the pier as a ship enters or leaves the harbor. Wear a jacket, because it is usually cool.

Early prospectors sought more in northern Minnesota than just iron ore. Some ignored iron ore finds in pursuit of precious metals such as gold. Others, such as the men who founded Minnesota Mining and Manufacturing, found other minerals they thought would make them rich.

Two Harbors attorney John Dwan and realtor H. W. Cable secured a supply of what they believed was corundum. They planned to crush it at Crystal Bay in order to produce abrasives and grinding wheels. In 1903, they established a plant and a home office for their company, 3M, in Two Harbors. They sold the first ton of their product in 1904 and learned it was a low-grade anorthosite. So, they leased an old flour mill on Duluth's waterfront and decided to produce sandpaper, instead.

However, in order to make sandpaper they needed garnet. Unable to obtain a domestic supply, the partners ordered half a boatload from Spain. Enroute to the United States the ship was caught in a storm. As the ship pitched in the heavy seas, kegs of olive oil rolled about the hold and were broken, draining into the ore bins. The oily garnet wouldn't adhere to the sandpaper, and 3M's first customers were a dissatisfied lot. Undaunted, the men secured more financing and moved their plant to St. Paul. The company continued to struggle, and for a while a share of stock was worth a glass of beer at a nearby tavern. From these humble beginnings grew one of Minnesota's largest corporations.

The story of Minnesota Mining and Manufacturing will be told in the new 3M Museum, located at 201 Waterfront Street. The company's original office is being renovated to its 1905 appearance. The project, which will cost more than $100,000, is receiving generous assistance from 3M.

The Lake County Historical Society Museum is certainly worth the modest admission fee. Located in the old railroad depot, the museum features displays of Lake County's past, including exhibits depicting railroading, logging, the iron ore industry, and pioneer life. The life of John Beargrease, the mushing mail carrier who is the namesake of the modern sled dog marathon, is also featured. Sports fans will be charmed by the exhibit of Two Harbors athletic teams.

Outside the museum two steam locomotives, the Mallet #221 and the Three Spot, represent the early years of northern Minnesota railroading. The Three Spot arrived in Agate Bay during the early 1880s via a scow and for over thirty years hauled ore from the mines to the docks. One of the largest steam locomotives in the world at 127 feet, 8 inches and about 1.1 million pounds, #221 saw service from 1941 to 1963. The DM&IR later purchased sixteen identical Mallet locomotives, of which only three remain.

The historical society also operates the lighthouse museum on the point east of the breakwall. The museum offers exhibits in the fog signal building and plans to open the small, white clapboard home that once housed the assistant keeper. The Agate Bay Light Station was constructed in 1892, and the Coast Guard controls its still-active light.

Also on the grounds is the pilot house from the ore carrier *Frontenac,* which ran aground at Silver Bay in 1979.

Shopping and such

Two Harbors has two business districts, one along Highway 61 and another downtown, six blocks from the highway. You can easily while away an afternoon investigating the shops and restaurants. Parking is readily available.

In Thomas Owens Park you can hear concerts on summer Thursday evenings and watch melodramas on Fridays in July. The Two Harbors Folk Festival is held the first weekend in July just outside of town at PAP Acres. Other events include the Harbor Fest and Carnival in late June, Heritage Days in July, and the Lake County Fair in August.

Tennis players will find courts about three blocks north of Highway 61 on State Highway Two. The nine-hole Lakeview Golf Course, dedicated in 1932, is nearby. Two Harbors also has a curling club and a hockey rink.

Lakeshore camping

The City of Two Harbors operates a 111-site campground east of town along Burlington Bay. Water and electricity are provided at 91 sites (of which 15 have sewer hookups) and 20 sites are for tenting only. You can snuggle into your sleeping bag and listen to waves breaking on the beach.

The *Edna G*

Built in 1896, the 102-foot tugboat *Edna G* was originally powered by a one-thousand-horsepower steam engine and consumed twenty-five tons of coal per week. She was retired from active service in 1981.

The tugboat served all 85 years at Two Harbors—except for two years of military service during World War I. The *Edna G* has been owned by the city since 1984.

Plans have been proposed to drydock the tug and open it for tours, but now she lies quietly moored in Agate Bay, not far from the mighty ore carriers she once assisted.

The gravel beach of Burlington Bay offers an excellent place to collect Lake Superior agates. Here, too, you can see how the agates were formed.

But first, a short geology lesson. Volcanic activity formed the rocky spine of the North Shore about 1,200 million years ago. Observers can discern the lava flow patterns in the Shore's rocky outcrops. The North Shore consists mainly of basalts, as well as some rhyolites and composite flows.

Gas pockets, which geologists call vesicles formed within the molten lava. Over time these gaps filled with minerals such as calcite, epidote, chlorite, and zeolite. The best known of these mineral deposits are referred to as agate and thomsonite (see Thomsonite Beach). Lake Superior agates are characterized by pink and white bands. The pinkish color is caused by the oxidation of trace amounts of iron.

At Burlington Beach you can see agates imbedded in the rocky outcrops. Most of these imprisoned agates are white. The agates you find in the gravel have been eroded from the volcanic rock. Most are small, although fist-sized and larger agates have been reported. A "wild" agate does not look like the polished specimens you see in rock shops. Often coarse material coats the characteristic pink. If the agate is broken, and many are, you can see the colored bands.

The best places for agate collecting are on the western end of the North Shore and are by no means limited to Lake Superior's beaches. A walk down nearly any gravel road in the Two Harbors and Duluth area will reward a picker with a handful of agate pebbles. Gravel pits in the area, especially south of Duluth in Carlton County, are favored collecting sites. Picking is productive all the way up the shore to Little Marais. Beyond that the agate supply diminishes.

Lake Superior Agates

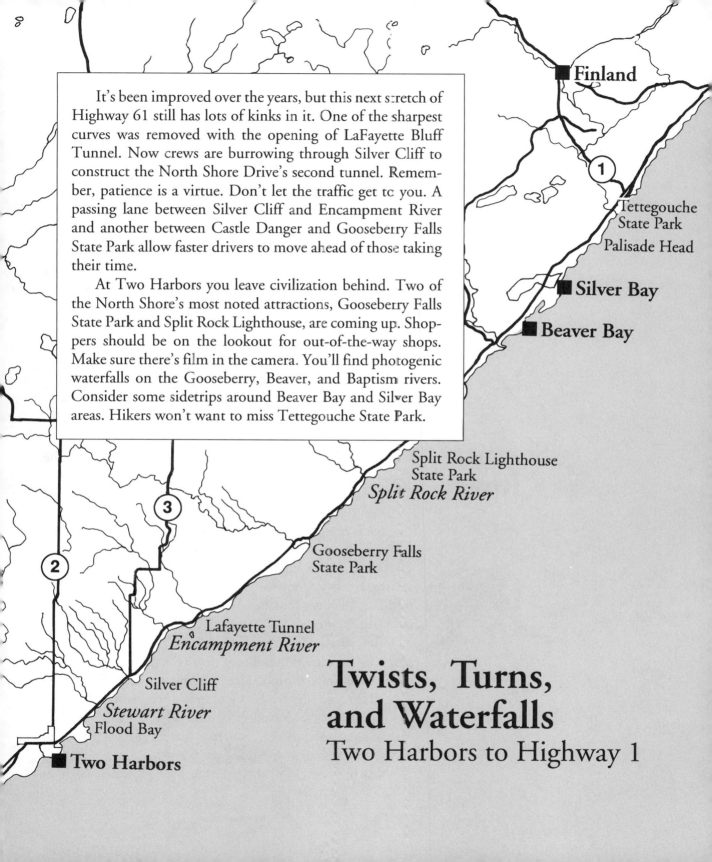

It's been improved over the years, but this next stretch of Highway 61 still has lots of kinks in it. One of the sharpest curves was removed with the opening of LaFayette Bluff Tunnel. Now crews are burrowing through Silver Cliff to construct the North Shore Drive's second tunnel. Remember, patience is a virtue. Don't let the traffic get to you. A passing lane between Silver Cliff and Encampment River and another between Castle Danger and Gooseberry Falls State Park allow faster drivers to move ahead of those taking their time.

At Two Harbors you leave civilization behind. Two of the North Shore's most noted attractions, Gooseberry Falls State Park and Split Rock Lighthouse, are coming up. Shoppers should be on the lookout for out-of-the-way shops. Make sure there's film in the camera. You'll find photogenic waterfalls on the Gooseberry, Beaver, and Baptism rivers. Consider some sidetrips around Beaver Bay and Silver Bay areas. Hikers won't want to miss Tettegouche State Park.

■ **Finland**

①

Tettegouche
State Park

Palisade Head

■ **Silver Bay**

■ **Beaver Bay**

Split Rock Lighthouse
State Park
Split Rock River

③

②

Gooseberry Falls
State Park

Lafayette Tunnel
Encampment River

Silver Cliff

Stewart River
Flood Bay

■ **Two Harbors**

Twists, Turns, and Waterfalls
Two Harbors to Highway 1

Flood Bay

MILEPOST 27 You may be surprised to learn that the North Shore has erosion problems. After all, there's nothing here but rock. But the rock is covered with a soil that varies from less than an inch to several feet in depth. When vegetation is removed, the exposed soil can wash away.

At Flood Bay, beachline erosion was stopped by using rock from the LaFayette tunnel project as riprap. It's now a desirable place to visit. Gooseberry State Park administers a nineteen-acre wayside at Flood Bay. Because the water is shallow for some distance from shore, large waves break and roll to create surf. Stone steps lead to the beach.

Wildlife watchers can check for activity at the beaver pond on the property. In the spring, look for migrating waterfowl since ducks need waysides, too.

Stewart River

MILEPOST 28 Old-time loggers learned the hard way that the Stewart River was no place to make a log drive. Prior to the turn of the century a massive log jam blocked the river for three years. When you look at this river, or any large North Shore stream, you can hardly imagine the environmental destruction wrought by those drives. First, the timber was cleared from valley hillsides, leaving behind bare, erodible slopes. Then each spring vast numbers of huge logs bounced downstream, gouging and scouring the streambed.

Time has healed the old wounds, and today conservation practices are incorporated into timber harvesting. You have to look carefully to find traces of early logging. The gravel deposits at some North Shore river mouths were formed by the erosion that followed large-scale clear-cutting. Anglers occasionally find ancient, sawn logs rotting along a riverbank or the aged remains of logging dams.

Nearly gone, too, are reminders of pioneers, such as

John Stewart, who settled here in 1865. People farmed along the North Shore well into the twentieth century, but most of the clearings and fields are now forests. Head inland on Lake County 3, which intersects with Highway 61 just east of Stewart River, and you can see some of the remaining North Shore farms.

County 3 follows the route of the Old North Shore Road. You can rejoin the highway at Beaver Bay or continue on the backroads all the way to Schroeder. The topography is surprisingly gentle much of the way, which no doubt encouraged residents to construct roads inland from the rugged lakeshore.

Silver Creek Cliff

MILEPOST 31 The sheer cliff just east of Silver Creek has long been a barrier to highway construction. Early roadbuilders detoured around the cliff, going inland with the Old North Shore Road. In the 1920s, however, a passage was dynamited across the rock face, allowing the highway to continue close to the shore. Steam bulldozers and wagons pulled by teams of horses removed the tons of rock.

The cliff became a prominent North Shore landmark, a thrill for tourists from the prairie. You can enjoy an outstanding view of the lake as you drive along the highway, although more than a few height-conscious travelers prefer to keep their eyes closed. By 1994 it will no longer matter, because all you'll see will be tile-lined tunnel walls.

Construction on the new $22 million Silver Cliff tunnel began in August 1991. When completed, the tunnel will be thirteen hundred feet long. The present roadway will be abandoned. A wayside will be constructed east of the tunnel with a pathway leading to the cliff.

Why a tunnel instead of a rock cut? One reason is the amount of material that must be excavated. The total amount of rock to be removed for the tunnel is estimated at 460,000 cubic yards. Highway engineers say an open cut would require the removal of 1.5 million cubic yards of material.

A North Shore Calendar

Tourists used to visit the North Shore only during July and August. The rest of the year you'd hardly see a soul. Gradually, people grew bolder and began venturing up the Shore at other times of year. They discovered the splendor of September and the stark beauty of January. Spring and late fall are still off-season for the tourist trade, but even then you'll find more souls seeking solitude than you might first expect. Anytime is the right time to visit the North Shore.

Spring

Spring is on its way when cross-country skiers start complaining about snow conditions. The trails on the south-facing slopes above the lake give out first, and the skiers head inland. Pretty soon the only places left to ski are the frozen inland lakes. Anglers start getting edgy.

Spring actually appears with the April rush of snowmelt in North Shore rivers. Waterfall watching is superb, though trails are muddy and slippery. Below the falls, steelhead anglers try their luck. In a couple of weeks the smelting season arrives, followed by the mid-May fishing opener.

Many of the tourist-related businesses don't open until late May or early June, but spring is an excellent time to go exploring because no crowds and no bugs are around. The weather ranges from shirt-sleeve pleasant to parka chilly. Often it is considerably warmer a short distance inland. Wear sturdy boots; you'll be walking through mud, snow, and puddles.

Summer

Summer shows up sometime in June, announced by a sudden attack of mosquitos and blackflies. The worst of the insect assault passes in a week or two, and modern bug repellant keeps them at bay. This may not be the Land of the Midnight Sun, but it is close. Certainly, the sun is reluctant to sink from the sky.

In June temperatures are still cool along the lakeshore, especially farther north. During July and August the Shore seems air-conditioned when compared to the steamy prairies, but occasionally the daily high temperature will creep over eighty degrees. You are most likely to encounter such a heat wave in late July and early August.

You are also likely to encounter the largest crowds in midsummer. Moms, Pops, and kids are out in full force. Travel without reservations and you may wind up sleeping in the car.

Autumn

In Grand Marais they say that autumn begins after Fishermen's Picnic, which is held the first weekend in August. They aren't kidding. Hints of fall color turn up in the woods, and gardeners start covering their tomatoes on cool nights. After Labor Day signs of autumn are clearly evident. Salmon start showing up in the rivers and grouse pick gravel along the roadsides.

Leaf lookers and grouse hunters start arriving in mid-September, about the time that the hawk migration comes into full swing. By mid-October the leaves are gone. Ponds and small lakes start skimming with ice at night. Flocks of snow buntings flutter up from the highway shoulders, heralding the first snow squalls. The parks and pathways are quiet, but beautiful. Deer hunters take to the woods during the first half of November. If you're out in the woods be sure to wear a blaze-orange or red coat or cap.

However, this is also when North Shore weather makes a nasty transition from fall to winter. You may want to find yourself a room with a fireplace and a view, and watch the stormy lake.

Winter

The North Shore winter officially begins on Thanksgiving weekend when ski runs open at Lutsen Mountains. Cross-country skiers and snowmobilers may not find groomed trails until December, but Christmas is always white up here.

Is it cold here in the winter? Of course it is, but even bitter, below-zero days are tolerable if you're properly dressed. And there's great stuff to do. You can downhill ski, cross-country ski, snowshoe, snowmobile, ice fish, dog sled, hay ride, and even shop. Lots of locals say winter is their favorite time of year.

Encampment

MILEPOST

32

As you cross the Encampment River, look out the window for a glimpse of the North Shore's past: a remnant of the original white pine forest. Less than one percent of Minnesota's original pine forest remains.

Although the surrounding area was logged during the 1890s, only a limited amount of cutting occurred in the Encampment forest. The property, which is private and not open to the public, has been preserved by the Encampment Forest Association. The forest has white pines more than two hundred years old, as well as ancient cedars. However, even this forest has been affected by the changes that have occurred around it since the North Shore was opened to settlement in 1854.

At that time, forest growth ebbed and flowed in response to fire. Through a process called forest succession, trees grew, matured, and eventually were replaced by another species. One of the first tree species to sprout after a fire is aspen, and white pine dominates a later successional stage. Today, forest management practices prevent the fires that continue the cycle.

Back in 1854, the hooved animals walking beneath the

Encampment pines would have been woodland caribou. Moose were uncommon on the North Shore, and white-tailed deer nonexistent. Logging, a warming of the climate, and indiscriminate shooting destroyed caribou and their habitat. Moose and white-tailed deer moved in. Today the Encampment forest supports a large herd of whitetails. They and snowshoe hares browse on the forest's new growth, snipping off the white pine and cedar seedlings. Researchers have built enclosures within the forest to keep out deer and give the young trees a chance.

A tree disease called blister rust, which came to North America from Europe, also affects the forest. Young white pine are especially susceptible to this disease, which is a primary reason why the species never returned following the early logging. Unfortunately, the North Shore's moist climate encourages blister rust, making it difficult for white pine to reach maturity. The disease also infects the big pines, causing dead tops.

Despite these changes, Encampment forest still offers a glimpse of the North Shore's past. Here we can visualize the Shore as it was seen by Indians and European explorers, when vast stands of pines covered the ridges.

LaFayette Bluff Tunnel

MILEPOST 33 LaFayette Bluff is named for a steamer that was wrecked here during a November storm in 1905. After the highway was constructed, the treacherous curve around the bluff gained a reputation for wrecks of another sort. The traffic accident rate was twice the statewide average. Adding to the danger, the roadway was slowly eroding. Little did most motorists know that nothing lay beyond the shoulder but a sheer drop.

Highway engineers were faced with a challenge. They could either blast a cut through the rock, as had been done in numerous locations along the Shore, or they could build a tunnel. Weighing the costs of acquiring additional highway right-of-way from nearby property owners and the environmental impacts, they decided to construct the first mined highway tunnel in the Midwest. The tunnel was opened to traffic in 1991.

The project wasn't cheap—totalling about $15 million. Nearly ninety tons of explosives were used during the excavation. Over two hundred thousand cubic yards of rock and other material were removed. The tunnel is 852 feet long, 55 feet wide, and 28 feet high. It has twelve-foot driving lanes, ten-foot shoulders, and a six-foot sidewalk. Continuous lighting in the ceramic-lined tunnel and a pavement monitoring system to detect icy roadway conditions make travel much safer than on the old highway.

Gooseberry Falls State Park

MILEPOST 39 You'll find a passing lane just before the Gooseberry River Bridge. Start slowing down when you reach the end of it because the bridge is one of the most congested areas on the Shore. Every North Shore river has waterfalls, but few are so readily accessible: at Gooseberry you can actually see and photograph the falls from the highway bridge. Just below the highway the river stair-steps along three cataracts, and you can look down the river valley for a hawk's-eye view of Lake Superior.

Not surprisingly, many of the seven hundred thousand annual visitors see little more of Gooseberry State Park. After twenty minutes of oohs, ahs, and clicking shutters, it's back into the car and on to the next roadside attraction. That's too bad. Gooseberry is a lovely park, and hikers quickly discover it takes but a few footsteps to put them far from the maddening crowd.

You'll have an excellent leg-stretching, hour-long walk if you take the trail upstream to Fifth Falls. You can follow the trail up one riverbank, cross the bridge above the falls, and walk back on the other bank. Just below the falls you'll see small caves that the river has carved into bedrock. No trails lead to the caves; and potential spelunkers should remember that if the river current gets the best of you while you're attempting to reach the caves, you could end up taking a fast and very bumpy ride to Lake Superior.

The river's rough and tumble character changes as it nears Lake Superior. It slows and widens into an estuary, a stretch with little gradient between the river and the lake. Nearly every North Shore river has an estuary (anglers call them lagoons), but the Gooseberry's is one of the largest along the coast. Perhaps that is why so many early explorers showed this river on their maps: this was a rare place where they could get off the lake and into quiet water, making it an ideal camping area. Some historians speculate that the river is named after the French explorer, Sieur des Groseilliers. Others say it is a translation of the Anishinabe name, *Shab-on-im-i-kan-i-sibi*, meaning "the place of gooseberries river."

The Nestor Logging Company established its headquarters there at the turn of the century and used the estuary as a log landing. The company dammed the river mouth and used narrow-gauge rail lines to haul logs from the backcountry. The railroad looped through what is now the campground to a high bank, where logs were dumped into the river. Once a sufficient stockpile of logs was collected, they were gathered into huge rafts, which were hauled across the lake to Ashland, Wisconsin, or Baraga, Michigan. A record-sized raft containing six million feet of logs was towed from Gooseberry to Baraga in eight days by the tug *Schoolcraft*. The *Schoolcraft* had passenger pigeons on board to release and send for help if it ran into trouble.

Danger always lurked in the early days of Great Lakes shipping. On April 29, 1903, the steamer *Belle P. Cross* lost the battle to a blizzard and sank just offshore near the river mouth. No lives were lost, but the ship and its cargo of railroad ties and poles were unsalvageable. You can often see the flags and vessels of divers over the wreck.

Not until after the Gooseberry country had been logged

was the area appreciated for its scenic value. The State of Minnesota acquired 368 acres including the river mouth, three waterfalls, and some shoreline during the late 1920s. Today's park was created by Civilian Conservation Corps (CCC) crews during the 1930s.

Those conservation crews constructed the park interpretive center along the highway and other structures, as well as roads and trails. Stone for the buildings was quarried in Duluth and East Beaver Bay. The CCC crews, directed by Italian stonemasons, cut and fitted the rock. An excellent example of their work is the three-hundred-foot stone wall that supports the parking area west of the river bridge.

The CCC camp, in operation from 1934 to 1941, stood on the west bank of the river above the highway bridge, an area now used for group camping. The young men who stayed there received thirty dollars per month, clothing, and medical and dental care. The men gained an average of eight pounds in six months eating the nutritious food that was provided for forty-six cents per day.

The CCC men also planted some of the vegetation now found in the park, such as the stand of conifers at the park entrance. However, the park's beautiful birch stands came naturally. They began growing after fires and logging early in the century destroyed the original tree cover. Observant hikers will notice that in some areas many birch are dead or dying. In fact, many North Shore birch stands may disappear in the future. Birch are short-lived trees, maturing in fifty to seventy years. North Shore stands are reaching maturity, and the older trees, damaged by drought during the 1970s, are dying off. Abundant deer herds browse on birch saplings, stifling new growth. Gradually conifers such as balsam and spruce, the trees next in line in forest succession, may replace the birch.

Gooseberry's birches are not the only familiar feature of the park that may soon disappear. The state highway department plans to replace the old steel bridge that spans the river. The new bridge will have a different alignment, which will eliminate present parking areas and the interpretive center. We hope that the new off-highway parking lots and visitors center will retain Gooseberry's charm. Judging by the concrete-and-mowed-grass approach that has characterized modern park improvements along the North Shore, we'd better keep our fingers crossed.

Beachcombers can reach the lake both east and west of the river. Careful inspection of the gravel at the river mouth could turn up an agate or two. Those looking for shoreline seclusion can hike to the mouth of Nelsen's Creek. Stay a respectful distance from the nesting herring gulls—they're feisty.

The Gitchi Gummi Trail, on the east side of the river, offers hikers vistas of the lake. Day hikers can follow the Superior Hiking Trail across the park and on to Split Rock State Park, a distance of about ten miles.

Shore-casting for lake trout used to be excellent at the river mouth, but a storm rearranged the gravel and eliminated the deep hole near shore. In the spring steelhead ascend the river to the base of Lower Falls. The Gooseberry isn't stocked with salmon, but a few run the river each autumn. Stream trout-fishing in the upper Gooseberry is nothing to write home about.

Gooseberry's campground, with seventy modern campsites, is among the most popular on the Shore. Make reservations to be assured a site. Facilities include flush toilets, showers, a campground shelter, and a trailer dump station. Winter camping is allowed, with drinking water, a heated shelter, showers, and flush toilets available. In addition, a group camp area is open during the warm months.

Picnickers can choose from three areas: one along the shoreline, another along the river, and a third near the park amphitheater. Or you could carry a sack lunch and eat at one of the six trail shelters located on the hiking trails.

Ousting Old Erick

In the fall of 1908 Erick Rosen rowed fourteen miles along the Lake Superior shore from Two Harbors to the Gooseberry River. There he found two things: an abandoned fishermen's cabin and love at first sight.

"I knew then that was where I wanted to be," he said many years later.

The Swedish immigrant, who worked as a longshoreman and logger, spent his spare time fixing up the small log cabin. When a stroke paralyzed his left leg and arm and he could no longer work in the woods, he moved into his home at the mouth of the Gooseberry. His neighbors spoke highly of him. Although crippled, he asked nothing of others and remained independent. Fishermen counted on the light in his window to guide them ashore. Summer tourists enjoyed his stories of early days along the North Shore.

Just after his seventieth birthday Rosen was ordered out of his cabin by the National Park Service. His home, as well as the homes of two fishermen, were slated for immediate destruction to make way for the new Gooseberry State Park. Despite criticism from the CCC workers and other fishermen, the bureaucrats were unflinching in their decree. Friends helped Old Erick move to his brother's home in Two Harbors. There, when interviewed by the *Duluth Tribune* in 1935, the grief-stricken old man summed up his feelings in one sentence.

"I just liked to hear the water," he said.

Family Skiing

Gooseberry State Park appeals to skiing families. Unlike at other parks, such as Tettegouche and Cascade, skiing need not be a strenuous backcountry excursion. Instead Gooseberry offers about fifteen miles of groomed trails through rolling hills. Short loops can be enjoyed by all ages.

Another plus is that Gooseberry is the first state park

along the shore with a ski trail system. Its proximity to Duluth and Two Harbors makes the park ideal for day trips, but its closeness to those cities doesn't mean that Gooseberry isn't wild. Skiers can count on seeing deer. Timber wolves, although seen less often, also frequent the park during the winter. In the evening, skiers may encounter great gray owls.

Ski pass required

A Minnesota ski pass is required on nearly every North Shore ski trail system. Although some skiers grumble when they purchase a pass, this "ski license" provides some of the funding for public trails. Trail upkeep is also supported by the volunteer efforts of local ski clubs and other funding sources.

Skiers aged sixteen to sixty-four must have ski passes and must carry them while skiing. Most trails where you must have a pass are marked with signs. Passes can be purchased from the DNR, county auditors, state parks, and participating local businesses. A three-year pass costs about the same as a good dinner and helps you get rid of calories instead of gaining them.

MILEPOST
43

The long gravel beach at the mouth of the Split Rock River makes a fine place for a picnic. You can find enough driftwood to build a small campfire on cool days. After you've eaten, you can look for agates along the beach or make a few casts into the surf.

Travelers have access to both sides of the river. A highway wayside is on the west bank. A quarter mile beyond the river to the east you can pull off the highway and drive back to the river on a segment of old roadway.

At the river mouth lines of old wooden pilings, part of a trestle, remain from turn-of-the-century logging operations. The Merrill and Ring Company employed as many as four hundred men to cut white and red pine. Logs were hauled

Split Rock River

on narrow-gauge rail lines to the lake. A hiking trail east of the river follows one of the old rail lines. After the logging was done, forest fires burned large areas of the forest. You can still find charred stumps from the giant pines.

The Split Rock River is probably best known by steelheaders. The barrier falls, which blocks the spring migration of the steelhead, is more than a half-mile upstream. The Split Rock has the distinction of being one of the few North Shore streams stocked with Atlantic salmon. The Minnesota DNR has discontinued its Atlantic salmon program, but spawning fish should continue returning to the river for a few years. Catching one in the river is largely a matter of luck, because they ascend at odd times. Look for them when the river rises following late-summer rains.

Shorecasters and ice anglers frequent the small harbor at the mouth of the Split Rock. In late winter they're trying for Kamloops rainbows, steelhead, and other species. Lake trout are the most common shore-casting catch. A couple of hundred yards east of the river a rocky point extends into the lake like a dock—a good place for casters to try their luck.

Take a quiet walk along the secluded shoreline east of the river. The land, part of Split Rock State Park, has both "official" hiking trails and quiet pathways. From the wayside on the west bank, a half-mile trail leads to an intersection with the Superior Hiking Trail. A small tributary to the Split Rock tumbles over a lovely waterfall near the trail crossing.

In the winter, skiers venture far up the river to view rock formations. This is backcountry skiing at its best. Those less adventurous can explore the groomed state park trails east of the river.

Well-named, indeed

Although the name Split Rock appears on maps dating back to 1925, no one knows for certain where it originated. Some say the river when viewed from the lake appears to split the rocky bluffs. Others have suggested that lines of light-colored anorthosite running through the darker diabase seem to "split" the rock. Another possible explanation is that a rock formation more than a mile upstream divides the river into two channels. The debate may never be settled, but obviously the river is well-named.

Spring comes slowly to the North Shore. It begins in March when wolves and coyotes croon their love songs. As the days get longer, sap starts running in the maple trees on Sawtooth Mountain ridges. White-tailed deer look for grass on sunny slopes of Highway 61 ditches.

All these signs indicate the waning of winter, but when spring arrives you can hear it. The music of running water plays as a winter's accumulation of snow melts and starts tumbling downhill toward Lake Superior. In the spring every North Shore gully carries a mad torrent. Rivers you can rock-hop across in August become brawling roller coasters of cold whitewater and rocks. Decaying leaves, branches, logs, and even winter-killed deer are flushed from the forest into the lake, providing the nutrients that are essential to Superior's food chain.

One could look at this watery fury and assume that fish are flushed from the rivers, too, but such is not the case. In fact, this is when steelhead ascend the streams to spawn.

Steelhead

Steelhead, seagoing rainbow trout, are native to the North Pacific. Like salmon, they are anadromous, which means that they spawn in rivers and spend their adult life in the ocean. Unlike salmon, steelhead don't die after spawning, but instead migrate back to the ocean and may return to the rivers and spawn again.

Steelhead were introduced to Lake Superior over one hundred years ago. Soon wild populations were spawning in most of the lake's tributaries. Although steelhead are stocked

Prince of the Rivers

in heavily fished areas today, the lakewide population consists largely of wild fish.

Spring-run steelhead are a sight to behold. Long and lean, the fish are bright silver with just a faint pink stripe along their flanks. After steelhead have spent some time in the river their rainbow trout coloration returns—a freckling of tiny black spots on the back and tail and a red "rainbow" stripe running from the cheek to the base of the tail. Hook-jawed spawning males have the most vivid colors; females remain silvery throughout the spawn.

Steelhead are among the strongest fish swimming in Superior's waters, which no doubt led to their successful adaptation to the lake. Undaunted by strong currents, they leap waterfalls in order to reach spawning gravel. Terrific leapers, steelhead can launch themselves four feet into the air to vault cascades. Their broad, powerful tails and muscular bodies allow them to swim upward in vertical columns of water for short distances.

When they reach the spawning grounds the female digs a nest, or redd, in the gravel. She lays her eggs there sporadically over a period ranging from a few hours to a day or more. One or more males fertilize the eggs. When the spawn is completed the steelhead slowly drift back to the lake. Even when headed downstream they face into the current, finning to hold their position. Occasionally they turn and swim a short distance downstream, only to turn again and face the current. Battered from their travels and the rigors of spawning, spawned-out steelhead often have scarred bodies and ragged fins. Some, especially males, do not survive.

Those who successfully return to the lake feed vigorously and regain strength. Like other predatory fish, they eat most anything. Their diet includes baitfish such as smelt, freshwater shrimp, and other aquatic life, and a surprising amount of insects. During the summer, land-born insects are a tremendous source of fodder for Lake Superior's trout and salmon. Hapless bugs are blown out over the lake by prevailing westerlies. Their bodies form rafts of flotsam which fishermen refer to as "bug slicks" on the lake. On calm days you can see the silvery backs of fish breaking the water as they feed upon the insects.

An adult steelhead in the lake has few enemies other than sea lamprey and anglers. For the young in the stream it's another matter. Steelhead spend the perilous first two or three years of their lives in the stream where they were born. There they must avoid larger trout, mergansers, mink, otters, kingfishers, and anglers. When they reach six or eight inches in length they smolt, a process of piscatorial puberty during which they develop a silvery sheen. As they migrate to the lake they must navigate a predatory gauntlet that includes loons, mergansers, lake trout, and salmon. A steelhead that survives to adulthood is indeed among the fittest of its species.

Of course, a fish with such noble characteristics makes a prime target for sport anglers. On the North Shore, you just aren't an angler unless you're a steelheader. Only a few anglers can make the grade, however. Catching a steelhead when the fish run the rivers in the spring requires finesse, persistence, and a measure of luck. The reward is worth the effort, because few freshwater species compare with a rambunctious steelhead on the end of a line.

Over the years North Shore steelhead anglers have developed a unique fishing style. They use expensive graphite fly rods, but don't cast flies with traditional flylines. Instead they use monofilament fishing line and lead sinkers to penetrate the fast currents where steelhead lurk. Their bait? A tiny piece of yarn, which is fastened to the hook with a snell knot. Newcomers to the sport, even if experienced anglers, are stymied by how a bit of fluorescent fluff can outwit a mighty steelhead, which generally range in size from three to ten pounds. The secret is that the yarn resembles a trout or salmon egg drifting in the current. Steelhead feed little while on their spawning run, but they will eat the eggs of their own kind or other species. In fact, steelhead eggs tied into marble-sized mesh sacks are another popular bait.

A novice may fish for one or two seasons before landing that first steelhead, but accomplished steelheaders are predators of heron-like efficiency. Countless North Shore fishing stories recall how the expert caught fish after fish while everyone else on the stream drew a blank. Perhaps this vulnerability to good anglers is one reason that North Shore steelhead numbers have declined. The stream mileage available to spawning steelhead along Minnesota's North Shore is limited, totaling less than two hundred miles, and the spawners are subjected to some of the heaviest fishing pressure in the state.

To help maintain the steelhead population many anglers choose to release the fish they catch, even though the trout are good to eat. Steelheaders brave fickle spring weather conditions not because they are hungry, but because steelhead are hard-fighting sport fish. By releasing fish to continue on their spawning run, anglers perpetuate both their sport and a wild species.

The Minnesota Department of Natural Resources recognized this philosophy when it adopted new regulations for steelhead in 1992. Biologists were concerned about a steelhead decline that had been in evidence for more than a decade. Elsewhere on Lake Superior and in the Pacific Coast fisheries, managers and anglers had learned that catch-and-release fishing practices have a tremendous positive impact on wild steelhead fisheries.

Beginning in 1992, Minnesota anglers are required to return to the water all steelhead measuring less than twenty-eight inches in length. The bag limit is one steelhead over twenty-eight inches, which is a trophy fish. The exception is that anglers can keep three stocked steelhead or Kamloops rainbow trout (another strain).

The stocked fish are marked with clipped fins. However, the "clippers" must measure at least sixteen inches in length.

Managers hope that the new regulations will help restore steelhead numbers.

These regulations signal the beginning of a new era for North Shore fishing. Time and again, Lake Superior sport and commercial fishermen have thought that the lake's supply of fish was limitless, and time and again they've been proven wrong. As tourism and recreational industries continue to grow on the North Shore, increasing pressure is placed on the area's fragile natural resources. Catch-and-release is one way by which people may continue to enjoy the North Shore's natural bounty, yet limit their impact on the resource.

Know your trout

Every summer hundreds of casual anglers drown worms in North Shore rivers to catch a fresh meal of trout. Many assume that the small trout they catch are brook trout, but the fish are more likely to be baby steelhead. In the past this error just meant that future generations of steelhead suffered an untimely end in a frying pan, but now a conservation officer may issue you a ticket if you have small rainbow trout in your possession.

Actually, it is easy to distinguish various trout species. Young rainbows are by far the most common inhabitants of the lower reaches of North Shore streams. Generally they are heavily spotted and have a pink or red stripe along their side. Young fish often have dark fingerprintlike markings, called parr marks, on their sides. Brook trout, which are more common in the upper reaches, are olive green in color and have wormlike markings on their backs. They have orange spots surrounded by blue halos along their flanks, and their fins are orange with prominent white edges.

If you have any doubt about the identity of the fish you catch, throw it back. A guide to fish identification is included in the Minnesota fishing regulations booklet.

How to release a fish

Studies have shown that upwards of ninety percent of the trout caught on artificial flies and lures survive when they are released. Trout caught on natural baits have lower survival rates, but careful anglers can expect the fish that they release will live. Most anglers feel a deep satisfaction watching fish they've caught swim away.

When landing a fish you intend to release, play it quickly. If possible, unhook the fish while it's still in the water. However, large fish such as steelhead are easier to handle in a landing net. Just be careful not to injure the fish with the net or in your hands. Also, don't allow the fish to flop around on the bank, where it could bruise itself.

If the fish is hooked deep in the mouth or gullet, cut your line. Fish have strong stomach acids, which will quickly dissolve a hook. Many anglers use barbless hooks to aid release.

Don't hold by the eyes or gills fish that you plan to release. Instead, cradle the fish with both hands. As you release the fish, gently hold it upright until it regains equilibrium. You'll know when the fish is ready to swim away. In streams, release fish in quiet areas, where they can rest before going into the current.

Split Rock Lighthouse State Park

MILEPOST 46 Split Rock Lighthouse, undoubtedly the best-known North Shore landmark, has been a star attraction since 1924 when the highway (then called Highway 1) was completed. The lighthouse remains popular, and is worth the price of two admission fees to get in.

Two admission fees? Yes. Some bureaucratic wrinkles defy ironing out. The Minnesota Historical Society administers the lighthouse site. However, the Minnesota Department of Natural Resources administers the surrounding lands, Split Rock State Park. Look at it this way: spending an afternoon at the lighthouse is still cheaper than taking the family to see a movie.

In fact, admission to the historic site includes a movie. A twenty-two-minute film about the lighthouse runs regularly at the small theater in the visitor center. Inside the center are engaging historic displays, a gift shop selling books of local interest, historical society offices, and the theater. The building offers, you might say, historical hors d'oeuvres, prepping you for the visit to the site.

You may choose a guided or an unguided tour of the lighthouse grounds. During the busy summer season, a half dozen or more interpreters are on duty. The lighthouse has been restored to its early 1920 appearance. Oak windows replaced aluminum ones. Glasswork was refitted or replaced. The tower base was given a paint job and time-wearied concrete was repaired. The historical society plans eventually to restore all buildings on the site to that time period.

The lighthouse beacon first shone in 1910. Demand for construction of the facility followed the particularly vicious autumn of 1905, when 215 lives were lost on the lake. A November storm wrecked the barge *Madeira* offshore from where the lighthouse now stands (tour guides will point out the site), and the steamer towing her, *Lafayette*, was lost in the rocks twelve miles west. However, Split Rock Lighthouse did not rise until America's men of steel flexed their political muscle. Following the turn of the century, millions of tons of iron ore steamed on freighters from the ports of Two Harbors and Duluth-Superior toward mills on the lower lakes. Shipping magnates found it cheaper to get the government to build lighthouses than to insure their fleets.

Construction began at Split Rock in 1909. It was no small task. At that time the only access to the site was by water. The only nearby human habitation was a Norwegian fishing camp called Little Two Harbors.

A derrick constructed at the top of the bluff hoisted building materials and equipment totaling 310 tons from an anchored barge. Needless to say, offloading required good weather. (Not until 1916, six years after the station was completed, was an elevated tramway built to haul goods to the station.) Project engineer Ralph Russell Tinkham also designed Rock of Ages Light at Isle Royale and later designed lighthouses on the Pacific Coast. He and immigrant work crews toiled on the project that first year until November, when they hiked through the woods to catch a logging train to Duluth.

The first keeper, Orren "Pete" Young, came to Split Rock in 1910 and stayed until retiring at age seventy in 1928. His duty was to ensure that the light didn't go out. He and two assistants rotated four-hour nighttime watches. During the day they took care of station maintenance. They kept everything up to snuff, because the keeper's Detroit superiors pulled surprise inspections.

The original light burned kerosene vapor and was so bright a person couldn't look at it. The Fresnel lens floated on 250 pounds of mercury and was turned by a giant clockwork mechanism. From April through December it flashed every ten seconds. The official range of the light was twenty-two miles, but it could be seen from Devil's Island on the outermost fringe of the Apostles—forty-five miles away. Fishermen said they could even see it from Grand Marais, a distance of sixty miles. The light still works, revolving on its mercury bearings, but a one-thousand-watt electric lamp has replaced the kerosene light.

The light's companion fog horn was blown when necessary. The horn had an official range of five miles, but the sounds that skipped across the water weren't reliable. Franklin Covell, the station's second keeper, once ran to the end of the dock and blew a tin whistle to prevent a fog-bound ore boat from running aground.

The station was originally administered by an agency called the Lighthouse Bureau, which was absorbed by the United States Coast Guard in 1939. When the Coast Guard took over, Split Rock was declared to be the most visited lighthouse in the country, and the tourist traffic hasn't let up since. On some busy days more than three thousand visitors arrive, and annual attendance tops two hundred thousand. Split Rock receives more visitors than either the Minnesota State Capitol or Fort Snelling.

The use of radar in shipping made lighthouses obsolete. In 1961 the fog signal was discontinued, and Split Rock was decommissioned in 1969. The lighthouse was deeded to the state and became a state park in 1971. In 1976 the Minnesota Historical Society took over administration of the twenty-five-acre lighthouse site.

The State Park

The sticker on your windshield gets you into Split Rock State Park, a sprawling area that includes two and a half miles of Lake Superior shoreline and a lengthy stretch of the Split Rock River. You can get lost here if you so choose. You can also mingle with as many people as you'd find in a suburban shopping mall. The park is crowded summer and fall, but nearly deserted the rest of the year. And that's just fine with the people who visit during the off-season.

Split Rock has a strategic location between Gooseberry and Tettegouche, which makes it an excellent headquarters for cross-country skiers. The park has about eight miles of regularly groomed trails, and a heated trail center provides comfort to both day skiers and winter campers. Larger groups use the trail center as a base so that everyone can ski at his or her own pace. Winter campers have no problem finding a solitary site, with a choice of cart-in campsites and the picnic area.

The cart-in sites, unique on the Shore, are popular during the warm months. Campers park their vehicles and then push their gear into the sites on large, wheeled carts. Nine of the twenty cart-in sites are along the lake.

Despite the fact that the lighthouse perches on a high

cliff, most park shoreline is accessible. If the lake is rough, the rocky beaches rumble like so many loose cannonballs. A series of hiking trails follows the shore, where there are four additional backpack campsites. Cross the highway and a trail climbs the ridge to an overlook and then loops back along an old logging trail. The Day Hill Trail, near the cart-in campsite, makes a shorter, stretch-the-legs loop. You can combine a lakeside walk with a climb to the summit of Day Hill.

You can still find a few foundations in the woods at the site of Little Two Harbors. Little Two Harbors was a camp for fisherman, not a settlement. No families lived in the rough, tar paper shanties.

As many as fifteen Norwegian herring fishermen operated out of Little Two Harbors from the early 1900s to 1924, when one fisherman bought the land where the shacks were located and tried to charge the others rent. Instead the fishermen moved on. A corundum mine, located on the rocky point west of the lighthouse, was opened by the Minnesota Abrasive Company in 1901 and sold to a fledgling 3M in 1903. Operations continued until 1906. A 1910 forest fire destroyed the mine shacks.

Shining on

Although Coast Guard regulations prevent its use on a regular schedule, Split Rock Lighthouse occasionally casts a light across Lake Superior. The light shines two or three times each month. It can often be seen on weekends, and is also lit for special events.

The lighthouse is a highly photogenic subject regardless of the season or the weather. Sites within the state park give the best angles , although with a telephoto lens it is possible to take photographs from the wayside on the highway.

Dramatic photos can be taken when the full moon rises above the lighthouse; the moon is in its best position during December and January. In the autumn, golden-yellow from the surrounding birches accents lighthouse photos.

Weatherwise photographers can also get interesting shots when the lighthouse is partially obscured by fog or snow.

Take It Easy

You can always spot the new arrivals. They have a glazed look from several hours of staring at asphalt. Like animals released from a cage, their movements are charged with pent-up energy. Many will be lucky if they are able to unwind before it's time to head home.

Unfortunately, they never realize what they've missed. Some, for instance, detest fog. They complain because the driving is slow and the views are obscured. A low-slung cloud smothers their vacation. Rather than feel angry or depressed, they should let the fog focus their attentions. Fog is refreshing and mysterious when you're following a woodland hiking trail.

The Shore is what you make of it. A hurry-up drive on Highway 61 is just that. Stop and get your shoes dirty. Did you come up here to listen to steel belts humming on the pavement or to hear seagulls? Slow down, relax and savor the Shore. That's what you're here for.

Beaver Bay

MILEPOST 50 A broad gravel spit lies at the mouth of the Beaver River. The land is private, but you can walk down there from the east side of the highway bridge so long as you don't litter or abuse the land. A new crop of agates washes up on the beach after every storm. This pleasant place has probably attracted people since humans arrived on the North Shore—an 1871 painting shows an Indian encampment there.

Beaver Bay is the oldest continuous white settlement along the North Shore. A townsite east of the Beaver River was platted and filed in St. Louis County on June 24, 1856. That same day a family of German settlers arrived at Beaver Bay on the steamer *Illinois*. They cleared land to build homes and farms and by 1859 began a sawmill, a gristmill, and a tannery. In 1871 another gristmill was built on the west bank of the river above the waterfall that you can see from the highway. Beaver Bay was then the population center of Lake County.

However, Beaver Bay, like other communities, lost in the development of northeastern Minnesota iron ore mining. Although a winter road was built between Beaver Bay and Lake Vermilion during the 1866 Vermilion Gold Rush, Beaver Bay did not become an iron ore port. The iron mining company begun by Beaver Bay founder Christian Wieland foundered. A railroad for shipping iron was built to Two Harbors instead of Beaver Bay. That community grew, and in 1886 the county seat was moved from Beaver Bay to Two Harbors.

Unlike other settlements, Beaver Bay didn't become a ghost town. Lumbering and commercial fishing provided an economic base at the turn of the century. But neither timber nor fish were inexhaustible. Fortunately, in 1924, as supplies of both dwindled, the new lakeshore highway was completed, and tourism quickly became an economic mainstay. Completion of the taconite plant at Silver Bay in 1952 brought many new people into the community.

Beaver Bay now has a population of about three hundred. Tourist-oriented businesses line the highway, so set aside some browsing time on your visit. Next door to the Beaver Bay Agate Shop is an extensive display of rocks and minerals, including Lake Superior agates and thomsonite. More businesses stand across the river in East Beaver Bay.

If you happen to travel the Shore during spring smelting season, don't miss the Beaver Bay smelt fry, held in the basement of the municipal liquor store. The smelt fry, an annual event for over three decades, is no small enterprise. It takes eighty-five volunteers per day to staff the operation. The recipe remains secret, but it begins with vigorously cleaned smelt. If you miss the smelt fry and still have an appetite for fresh fish, inquire locally about herring. Fishing charters serve those who'd like to catch their own meal.

John Beargrease

Every winter, mushers in the John Beargrease Sled Dog Marathon bring their teams to the small Indian cemetery in Beaver Bay to pay tribute to a man buried there. John Beargrease carried mail along the North Shore from 1879 to 1900, using a dog team during the winter. He and other mail carriers followed lakeshore trails, traveling on the ice whenever possible. A wagon road completed between Duluth and Grand Marais in 1899 put them out of business—stages carried the mail faster.

Beargrease died of tuberculosis in 1910. To visit the cemetery where he is buried, turn north on Lake County 4 and take the first left. A totem pole marks the cemetery.

Silver Bay

MILEPOST 54 It began with rumors during the World War II years. Northern Land Company and Lake Superior Land Company were buying up property east of Beaver Bay for a new resort, the locals said. The real estate people paid cash and didn't talk. In 1946, the cat was let out of the bag: Silver Bay would be the site of a new taconite processing plant.

During a half century of mining activity, the Mesabi Iron Range provided raw material for the steel that built America's industrial power. However, the Mesabi's high-grade ore was a finite commodity; one did not need a crystal ball to predict that it would eventually run out. Taconite, however, a hard rock containing low-grade iron, was found in tremendous quantities on the one-hundred-mile-long range. State geologist Newton Winchell had identified and named taconite in 1892 and an experimental processing plant had operated in Babbit during the early 1920s, but production was considered economically infeasible.

Dr. E. W. Davis, head of the University of Minnesota's Mines Experiment Station, devoted his forty-five-year career to researching taconite production. During the 1930s his work had progressed to a point that mining companies were willing to gamble on the hard rock. Reserve Mining Company was formed in 1939, with steel companies Republic and Armco Steel as controlling interests. Company officials then successfully lobbied to have taconite taxed at a lower rate than other ores.

A Lake Superior site such as Silver Bay made an excellent location for a plant, because taconite processing required large amounts of water. However, the company needed to build not only a plant but also a town to house workers. Prior to construction, Reserve undertook sociological studies to determine what sort of people would settle in the community. Construction began in 1951, and families began moving into the new homes in 1952. The city was self-contained, with schools, a library, a shopping center, and recreational facilities. The plant started operation in October 1955, and the following April the steamer *C. L. Austin* left Silver Bay with the first load of pellets—10,800 tons.

The taconite production process involves many steps. Crude taconite, containing 24 percent iron, is hauled forty-seven miles by rail from Reserve's Babbitt mine to the plant. Machines process it into marble-sized pellets of 65 percent iron, which are shipped on lake carriers to steel mills on the lower lakes. Although past production has topped 10 million tons of pellets annually, the current rate is less than 4 million tons. The open pit mine in Babbitt is now ten miles long and a half mile wide.

Taconite processing produces vast quantities of powdered waste rock called tailings. Initially those tailings—averaging sixty-seven thousand tons a day—were dumped into Lake Superior, where, it was assumed, they would settle to the bottom. Most did, forming a giant delta off the plant. However, some particles remained suspended in the water.

Commercial fishermen noticed that the lake water developed a greenish tint and that particles collected on the mesh of their nets.

Environmentalists began criticizing Reserve during the 1960s, expressing concern that the tailings contained asbestos fibers that would harm people drinking Lake Superior water. The United States Justice Department filed suit against the company in 1972. During the next few years the Reserve Mining case made a continuing front-page story in Minnesota newspapers. In 1978 Reserve was permitted to build an onland disposal site at a place called Milepost 7.

Reserve spent $370 million to build the disposal facility and improve its air emissions. Milepost 7 opened in 1980. The disposal site is 675 feet higher and several miles inland from the plant. Tailings are pumped through two twenty-four-inch pipelines to the six-square-mile disposal basin. Water used in the process is recycled.

The early 1980s devastated northeastern Minnesota economically. Layoffs at Reserve began in 1981. By 1983 the company's original workforce of 3,100 had been pared to 950. In 1986, following further layoffs, Reserve closed. Unemployment throughout Lake County soared, and lifetime residents were forced to move elsewhere to find work. Silver Bay homes sold cheaply, but found few buyers.

In 1989 Cyprus Minerals Company was awarded the $680-million plant in bankruptcy court for $52 million. The company renovated the plant, reopening in 1990. Although it employs fewer workers than Reserve did during its heyday, Cyprus is a major economic force on the North Shore. Tours of the facility are available during the summer. You can get a good view of the plant from an overlook reached via a short hiking trail in town.

To reach the community of Silver Bay, turn inland at the stoplights. The former Reserve country club is now a scenic nine-hole municipal golf course. You will cross the river four times in the course of play.

During the winter the Silver Bay hockey arena is the busiest place in town.

Local clubs maintain an extensive and scenic system of snowmobile trails, connecting North Shore corridor trails. A groomed ski trail system links with Tettegouche State Park via the Palisade valley. Trailhead for the Northwoods Ski Trail is on Penn Boulevard. This ski system is an underutilized gem. Even ATV riders can find trails here.

Mountainous country surrounds Silver Bay. Steep hillsides give way to palisades. In places you'll find alpine-like boulder fields. A paved scenic drive goes through the town of Silver Bay and follows Lake County 4 to Highway 1. Along the way you'll pass Lax Lake, popular with local swimmers and one of the few along the Shore where you can catch sunfish. Public access off County 4 leads to it.

Offshore

One of the North Shore's better boat access sites is just west of Silver Bay off Highway 61. You can launch most trailerable craft at Bayside Park. A solid dock separates two ramps, and a breakwater protects the launching area. This is a good place for an inexperienced Lake Superior boater to learn the ropes.

This area offers generally good fishing, especially when the coho salmon move in during midsummer. Prominent landmarks such as Split Rock Lighthouse and Palisade Head lie within reasonable cruising distance. Boaters and landlubbers alike will enjoy the park's picnic area.

The North Shore Corridor Trail

Winter is an especially scenic season on the North Shore. The somber greens of the pines and firs contrast with their snowy mantles, and Lake Superior's icy blue waters provide visual relief found nowhere else in Minnesota's wintry landscape. It's no wonder that snowmobilers are discovering this area and the 153-mile North Shore Trail, which runs from Duluth to Grand Marais.

The trail offers riders many different options. You can spend a weekend based in one North Shore community, explore the local trail system, and return to the same motel each night. You can also tour the length of the trail. Another option is to follow one of the trails leading to the Iron Range. You could spend every winter weekend on the North Shore and never run out of trails to explore. Let's start at the trail's beginning, a parking lot on Duluth's Martin Road, and look at the possibilities along the entire route.

Duluth to Two Harbors

From Martin Road the North Shore Trail leads inland, or away from Lake Superior. The trail parallels the big lake, but lies behind the high ridge rising up from the shoreline. Spur trails offer scenic vistas of Superior, but the only place where you'll see the lake from the main trail is as you enter Grand Marais. However, being away from the lake offers an advantage: Lake Superior moderates the shoreline climate. Usually, you'll find more snow a few miles inland. This snow also lasts longer in the spring.

Six miles from the parking lot you'll reach a picnic shelter, the first of many along the trail. The shelters are three-sided structures with fire rings, picnic tables, and toilets. The outdoor toilets are designed with winter wanderers in mind—the seats have cozy plastic risers!

The first cutoff is the new Taft Trail, which goes past Island and Boulder lakes (both known for good fishing) and on to the tiny community of Alborn. From there it goes north to connect with the western end of the Taconite Trail on the Iron Range.

Farther up the main trail another new route, the Pequaywan Lake Trail, extends fifty-five miles, joining the Taconite Trail at Hoyt Lakes.

Just after crossing County Highway 2, you'll see the spur trail that leads south to Two Harbors. There you'll find accommodations, fuel, and a variety of restaurants. Two

Harbors has snowmobile routes on streets marked with orange diamonds. The speed limit is ten miles per hour on the streets, and you must stop at all intersections. A parking lot for snowmobilers lies just north of town.

Two Harbors to Finland

Although the stretch from Duluth to Two Harbors certainly isn't suburbia, once you cross Highway 2 you're definitely in the woods. By the way, those big tracks you see plunging off through the trees weren't made by horses. This is moose country. The huge doglike tracks that occasionally follow the trail are timber-wolf prints.

If you want to see some wildlife, head south on the spur that leads to Gooseberry Falls State Park. A large deer herd winters in the park, and you can often see them from the trail. Famous Gooseberry Falls is frozen now, but it's still pretty. From the Gooseberry spur it's a fairly long haul—more than twenty miles—to the trail leading into Silver Bay and Beaver Bay. The local trail system here is among the more scenic along the North Shore, offering several views of the lake. You can also ride through Tettegouche State Park. You'll pass a couple of small lakes, but riding isn't allowed on them. If you want to try ice fishing, you'll have to walk out to your fishing hole. Both lakes contain northern pike.

Silver Bay doesn't allow snowmobiles on the streets, but a system of trails will get you around town. You can fuel yourself and your sled, and find a place to stay. Not far away is Finland, which also has food, fuel, and accommodations. Just outside Finland on County Road 7 is a parking area.

Finland to Grand Marais

Twenty miles out of Finland you'll come to the Tomahawk Trail, a favorite of many riders. The Tomahawk tracks seventy-five miles through the heart of the Superior National Forest to Ely. Continuing up the North Shore Trail you'll come to the spur leading to Schroeder. This trail's claim to fame is the longest bridge on the North Shore Trail system—a 142-footer spanning the Cross River. Schroeder offers gas and food, and limited parking is available.

The next spur goes to Bluefin Bay Resort in Tofte. Shortly after crossing the Temperance River you'll see a high promontory called Carlton Peak, which rises like a mountain above Tofte. Although Tofte offers food and lodging, no gasoline is available. In this area you'll find accommodations ranging from condos to bed-and-breakfasts. The smart sledder will call ahead for reservations, especially on weekends. Remember, this is ski country!

At Tofte you can also get on the Lutsen trail system. You can follow the lakeshore to Lutsen or take one of several spurs back to the North Shore Trail. At the Poplar River you'll cross a portion of the new championship golf course. Snowmobiles, strictly prohibited from the course, must follow the marked trail.

But let's return to the North Shore Trail. Beyond the Sawbill the trail follows the valley of Sixmile Creek. Not long after you pass one of the Lutsen spur trails you'll come to the trail shelter at Barker Lake. This trail shelter was the site of Kid's Village during the summer of 1990 when the Rainbow Family held their national gathering here. (The Rainbow Family is a group of latter-day hippies. During the peak of the gathering more than fifteen thousand of them roamed these woods.) Another five miles down the trail you'll cross the Caribou Trail, where there is a parking area.

Follow the next spur trail to Lutsen or to Cascade River State Park. Cascade is another good place to see deer or, if you're really lucky, a wolf.

Following the North Shore Trail you'll soon reach Pike Lake. A trail shelter stands on the lakeshore, and you can snowmobile on the lake. However, watch out for slush. Bury a machine here or on any other lake and it may take you hours to get it out. Generally, slush conditions are the worst during years when heavy snow falls early. The weight of the snow pushes down on the ice. Often the problem gets worse when ice anglers start drilling holes. If you are unsure about the slush conditions, inquire locally. To be safe, follow the tracks left by others.

After Pike Lake, the next spur is the Bally Creek Road, which leads to Devil Track Lake and the extensive Gunflint trail system. One could easily spend a weekend exploring the Gunflint trails. You can go all the way to Saganaga Lake on the Canadian border. Reliable rumor says the Canadians are considering a trail, along an old railroad grade from Sag to Thunder Bay. For now, however, Sag is the end of the line. Perhaps the favorite Gunflint route is the loop from Devil Track Lake to Poplar Lake.

Ice fishing is a popular winter activity on the Gunflint. Lakes are easily accessible by snowmobile—many are right on the trails. The best winter fishing is usually for lake trout and stream trout. You can get a guide to the local lakes from the DNR office in Grand Marais.

The North Shore trail concludes at a parking lot on the outskirts of Grand Marais. Snowmobiles are allowed in town. Travel slowly, stop at intersections, and follow marked routes. Grand Marais has several lodging facilities, restaurants ranging from casual to fine dining, and fuel. Winter trade has picked up during recent years, so it's a good idea to get advance reservations. Want to know a great way to make your stay special? Get up early and watch the sunrise over Lake Superior. If you're not an early bird, sunsets over the Sawtooth Mountains are equally spectacular.

Grand Marais and beyond

Plans have been made to extend the North Shore Trail all the way to Grand Portage on the Canadian border. For now, however, you must bushwhack to Grand Portage on ungroomed trails. Get directions from someone in Grand Marais. Better yet, have them draw you a map. Be sure to fuel up before you leave, because it's more than forty miles.

Grand Portage has a groomed snowmobile trail system that leads right to Grand Portage Lodge. Unless you know the country, be sure to leave Grand Portage well before dark for your return to Grand Marais. Otherwise you could end up lost in a maze of unmarked trails.

Final notes

The North Shore Trail is groomed three times during the week and on Saturday nights by the DNR and three local clubs contracted by the state. The entire trail and most spurs are groomed by Tucker Snow Cats with Trailmaster drags.

Snowmobilers share the trail with dog mushers during the John Beargrease Sled Dog Marathon in January. The trail stays open during the dog race, but snowmobilers should keep an eye out for the teams.

Palisade Head

MILEPOST 57 The view from Palisade Head is spectacular. On clear days you can see miles across the lake to the Apostle Islands and up the shoreline to the Sawtooth Mountains.

Until recently the highway department managed Palisade Head. Now it is part of Tettegouche State Park. The view from Palisade is just a three-season attraction because the winding road to the summit is not plowed during the winter.

The volcanic rock of Palisade Head is rhyolite, as is the rock at Shovel Point to the northeast. The cliffs, popular with climbers, drop 320 feet to Lake Superior. Small islands poke through the water offshore. All along the shoreline you can find small caverns carved into the rock.

Peregrine falcons nest nearby. Use your binoculars to look for them and other raptors.

During the summer a meander through the scrub growth should produce a handful of blueberries.

On the rocks

Throughout the summer, rock climbers test their skills on Palisade Head. These cliffs and those on Shovel Point and Carlton Peak are popular with climbers because of their accessibility. However, numerous out-of-the-way cliffs are scattered throughout the backcountry. In the winter, climbers seek out ice formations in North Shore river canyons.

The Lake Superior coast attracts climbers because it is the only place in the Upper Midwest where you can make multi-pitch climbs—longer climbs that involve the use of more than one rope. One of the nearest places you can find similar climbing is Devil's Tower, Wyoming.

If you catch the climbing bug, seek professional instruction and accompany experienced climbers. This sport can be hazardous if you don't know what you're doing.

North Shore Birding

Go to the Hawk Ridge overlook on Duluth's Skyline Drive any day during September and you'll see them. They're quiet, statuesque, gazing skyward with their trusty binoculars, searching for the migrating hawks for which this ridge is named.

Hawk Ridge is certainly the best known birding location on the North Shore, but Superior's coast and the inland forests have much more to offer birders. Along the Shore various elements of geography and climate collide and merge, providing habitat for both resident and migrant bird species.

Specifically, on the North Shore the coniferous boreal forest of the North meets the leafy transitional forests that extend north from the prairie. The bulk of Lake Superior moderates the climate and acts as a wall for migrating birds, which then follow the North Shore. Human activities such as logging, settlement, and small-scale agriculture provide a complex mosaic of bird habitats. Finding the birds you seek becomes a matter of knowing where and when to look for them. On the Shore, birding is most easily focused on the change in seasons.

Spring

In February, the acrobatic mating flights of the ravens above Highway 61 are an early sign of spring. Inland, the calls of mating saw-whet and boreal owls pierce the silence of winter nights, with activity peaking in March and April. Around the same time herring gulls start wandering north, congregating near open leads in the ice.

Lengthening days and melting snow trigger a flood of northbound migrants. Flocks of migrant ducks, especially diving species, can be seen on the lake. Mergansers, loons, and others congregate near river mouths to feed on spawning smelt while they wait for the frozen inland lakes to open. Small shoreline ponds at Flood Bay and Paradise Beach attract an ever-changing parade of waterfowl, including mallards, black ducks, and ring-necked ducks.

In the forest, the ruffed grouse drum. If you stand quietly on the edge of a clearing in the evening, you can watch the crazy, twittering flight of mating woodcock. The woods resonate with mating and territorial calls of a variety of birds, including the haunting song of the white-throated sparrow. This is a good time to look for birds along woodland paths; they are more easily seen due to the absence of foliage, and no biting insects will distract you.

Summer

The long days of summer are the best time to look for songbirds that nest in the boreal forest, especially warblers and flycatchers. More than twenty species of warblers, including the Connecticut and Cape May, nest in the North Woods. Flycatchers you may see here include the yellow-bellied and the alder flycatchers.

If you drive the backroads during the summer, you're likely to happen upon a mother grouse and her brood. In early summer the chicks are but tiny puffballs. Later they begin to resemble miniature versions of their mother. Paddle a canoe on inland lakes and you'll see ducks and loons with their young. On quiet summer evenings you can hear loons calling across the lakes.

The Superior National Forest also has nesting bald eagles, although fewer than in the Chippewa National Forest in north-central Minnesota. The Forest Service district offices in Tofte and Grand Marais can help you locate eagles. Most likely you'll need a canoe to get the best view.

By August, a keen observer will notice signs that autumn is approaching. At dusk you'll see migrating nighthawks pursuing insects as they follow the lakeshore south. Duck families make training flights to prepare for their upcoming journey. Some shorebirds, as well as a handful of hawks, begin their migration.

Fall

Autumn is the best season for North Shore bird watching. Birds of many species funnel along the North Shore in their southward migration. Best known are the raptors, which make an annual appearance in the skies above Hawk Ridge. The hawk migration peaks in September and October, but is wholly dependent upon weather. Hawk watchers prefer cold fronts with northwest winds. A series of foggy days will ground the migrants and allow close-range viewing. Every year there are days when ten thousand or more hawks are counted at Hawk Ridge, with the one-day record being thirty-four thousand birds. Common species include sharp-shinned and broad-winged hawks, kestrels, turkey vultures, and northern harriers.

Hawk Ridge is the best, but by no means only, hawk-viewing area. You can see hawks from any ridge above the lake. Grouse hunters and leaf lookers often see various woodland hawks in the backcountry. Clear-cuts are always an excellent place to watch for raptors and other bird species.

Other migrants also follow the natural corridor along the North Shore. You can see tremendous numbers of common birds such as robins, warblers, flickers, and blue jays. Flocks of crows follow the lakeshore. At times you can see migrating Canada and snow geese, although the western Minnesota prairies are a far better place to look for migrating waterfowl.

In October after the leaves have fallen, flocks of snow buntings and juncos brighten the roadsides. Late migrants include red-tailed and rough-legged hawks, bald eagles and occasional golden eagles. November and December are when waterfowl called sea ducks appear on Lake Superior, primarily in Cook County. Old-squaw and scoters are most common, although harlequin ducks are occasionally sighted. More rare are Barrows goldeneye and king eiders.

Winter

The best time to look for many resident birds is when there's snow on the ground. Common visitors at the bird feeder include boreal chickadees, pine grosbeaks, crossbills, and purple finches. Investigating the suet will be downy, hairy, and black-backed woodpeckers, as well as gray jays. Northern shrikes may prey on birds attracted to the food supply.

Often only the croaking of ravens breaks the stillness of the winter woods. In some years, however, large numbers of owls, the great gray, snowy, boreal, and hawk, invade the North Woods. Winter is also a good time to explore jack pine and spruce stands for spruce grouse. A bird of the boreal forest, spruce grouse nearly disappeared in Minnesota in the years following early logging. They have since become relatively common as the second-growth northern forests have matured.

Places to look

You can enjoy looking for birds at many locations along the North Shore. Beginning at Duluth, Lester River and Brighton

Beach are good places to look for fall migrants. Every autumn, Duluth birders count migrants other than hawks at the Lakewood Pumping Station. Stony Point also attracts a variety of species.

A large herring gull colony is located on Knife Island, offshore from Knife River. The sheltered waters of Agate Bay provide good viewing in Two Harbors. Mountain ash and crab apple trees near Burlington Bay attract fall flyers. In the winter, you can look for owls near the fields on County Highway 2 north of Two Harbors.

At Beaver Bay, the sewage treatment settling ponds along County Road 4 draw waterfowl both spring and fall. Similar ponds behind the condos at the Lutsen ski hill are also duck magnets. You may see anything from robins to ruffed grouse feeding on crab apple and mountain ash trees in the Tofte and Lutsen area.

Good Harbor Bay is a reliable place to see old-squaw and scoters in late autumn. However, the Grand Marais harbor offers by far the best place for waterfowl watching, with a summertime flock of Canada geese and a colony of herring gulls. During migrations you are likely to see a variety of ducks. The pebble beaches attract a variety of shorebirds and a mixed flock of mallards and black ducks winter there.

Paradise Beach is another good place to look for old-squaw, scoters, and goldeneyes. The offshore islands support nesting herring gulls. Sewage treatment ponds at Grand Portage are good places to find shorebirds and waterfowl.

Inland, only your imagination and your knowledge of the country limit you. Birders look for spruce grouse during the winter in the coniferous forests about twenty-five miles north of Two Harbors on County 2. Side roads off the Gunflint Trail, particularly the Lima Mountain Road, are good places to look for nesting birds.

About the gulls

Two common species of gulls live along the North Shore.

Ring-billed gulls nest only in the Duluth area, and herring gull colonies are found in several locations along the Shore. The two species resemble each other; the herring gull is somewhat larger and has a red spot on its yellow bill, the ring-billed gull has a black ring around the tip of its bill. It takes gulls several years to reach maturity. Immature gulls of both species are brownish gray; they do not acquire their characteristic white plumage until their third year.

Gulls travel to the Atlantic and Gulf coasts for the winter, but they'll hang around as long as food is available. Fish-processing operations in Grand Marais attract a large winter flock. Glaucous and Thayers gulls occasionally show up among the winter birds, and other gull species make rare appearances.

The peregrine returns

The decimation of raptors due to DDT contamination was one of the most publicized environmental stories of the 1960s. The birds of prey laid eggs, but the shells were so thin that they broke before the young hatched. The DDT ban gave the birds a chance to come back, and some species, including the bald eagle, have done remarkably well.

However, the most poignant success story is that of the peregrine falcon. Eliminated throughout much of its range due to DDT, the peregrine seemed unlikely ever to return. Fast enough to catch a duck or pigeon in flight, the peregrine elicits awe from anyone who has seen it.

Restoring the peregrine to its natural habitat has proved a massive task. The bird prefers to nest on high cliffs. Young birds are released in a suitable area—ranging from natural bluffs to bridges and skyscrapers. The young are carefully monitored until they achieve the freedom of flight. Then biologists cross their fingers and hope that the birds will survive and return to the release site to nest.

Falcons have been released at various locations along the North Shore, and the project has met with some success. In recent years a pair has nested at Palisade Head, and reports have come in of falcons in other places. Although you may see peregrines near any rocky crag along the Shore, Palisade Head is the best place to look for them. The nest sits on a cliff ledge about one hundred yards northeast of the parking lot. You may see the birds hunting or perched in trees.

Tettegouche State Park

MILEPOST 58 For many years, the highest waterfall in the Minnesota state park system was 70-foot High Falls on the Baptism River, but now that Pigeon River, with its 130-foot waterfall, is becoming Minnesota's newest state park, there will be a new claimant to that record. Since the Pigeon forms the border with Ontario, High Falls on the Baptism must be called the highest waterfall entirely within Minnesota.

High Falls was the star attraction of the former Baptism River State Park, which was essentially a glorified wayside. During the 1970s the state acquired an area inland, called the Tettegouche Camp. This lead to the establishment of Tettegouche State Park in 1979.

The lumbermen of the Alger-Smith Logging Company brought the name Tettegouche with them from eastern Canada. On the shores of a lake they called Mic Mac, after a New Brunswick Indian tribe, they established a logging camp. Nearby Tettegouche, Nicado, and Nipisiquit lakes were named for New Brunswick rivers.

In 1910 the camp was sold to a group of Duluth businessmen as a private retreat. They built a log lodge and other buildings at Mic Mac Lake. In 1921 Clement K. Quinn bought out the other partners. He preserved the area's wilderness character and acquired additional land. Fifty years later he sold the property to John and Karl DeLaittre, who continued to preserve it. Subsequent negotiations with the state and the Nature Conservancy led to public ownership of the land and the establishment of the state park.

The Tettegouche backcountry is one of Minnesota's most spectacular landscapes, a mountainous hardwood forest known to ecologists as the North Shore Highlands. It contains old-growth stands of maple and yellow birch, as well as ancient cedar swamps. In addition, one ridge is forested with northern red oak, a tree rarely seen on the North Shore. In autumn black bears travel up to fifty miles to feed on acorns along the ridge. Researchers have found that these bears enter hibernation later than other northern Minnesota bears and also start bearing young earlier in life.

Equally spectacular are the park's lakeshore holdings, which include Palisade Head and the Little Palisades—better known now as Shovel Point. You can walk out on the point from the park headquarters on Highway 61, following a trail to an overlook. Some naturalists believe that the trail and overlook are an intrusion on Shovel Point's natural beauty. Park officials counter that channeling foot traffic on the trail—annually the park receives 220,000 visitors, many of whom take the trek to the point—has protected fragile vegetation. Still, development rears its ugly head in other places in the park. Bridges and boardwalks have been built on riverside paths, and even the park road and campground were carved from an area that was an unbroken forest a few years ago.

From the main trailhead you can walk in several directions. The trail to High Falls is the most popular. You can cross the Baptism on a new bridge constructed for the Superior Hiking Trail and then take a stairway to the base of the falls. A trail leads downstream to Two Steps Falls and then back to the trailhead via the campground. The entire excursion takes an hour or more. For a somewhat longer hike, make the climb to the Lake Superior overlook, where you can look down the river valley to the lake.

If you want to explore Tettegouche Camp, plan on a full day of hiking. Wear sturdy footgear, and carry lunch and a canteen. Be prepared for rugged hiking.

The Tettegouche Camp buildings are at Mic Mac Lake. Plans have been made to restore the structures and open them for overnight rental beginning in 1993. You can walk into the camp on a service road which begins at an unmarked parking lot along the Lax Lake Road (Lake County 4). It's about a mile and a half from the parking lot to the camp. Looping sidetrails offer an opportunity to explore high ridges above the lakes. The hardwoods make an absolutely stunning show in late September.

Fishing at Tettegouche

The lakes offer fishing opportunities, although you'll have to carry in either a canoe or a belly boat. Northern pike and yellow perch inhabit the three larger lakes, and Nipisiquit also contains some walleyes. Nicado used to contain trout, but they disappeared not long after the park was opened.

The Baptism River is a popular fishing stream, especially when the chinook salmon are running in the fall. Most fishing pressure is between the highway bridge and the Cascades, a waterfall about a half mile upstream. The Baptism can be crowded, especially on autumn weekends, but you can usually find a place to fish. Farther upstream the river contains brook and brown trout.

A thirty-four-unit rustic campground is located about a mile inland from Lake Superior on a ridge above the Baptism River. It has no hookups but does have a modern shower building. Make advance reservations to assure a place during peak summer and fall months.

Skiing at Tettegouche

Experienced cross-country skiers will find a winter wonderland on the twelve miles of groomed trails in Tettegouche. The trail system starts at the main trailhead and goes inland. You can also gain access to the trails from the parking lot on the Lax Lake Road.

Tettegouche may be too much for beginners—all trails

are at least moderately difficult, and the shortest loop is over four miles long. Trails are groomed for both traditional skiing and ski-skating.

If you have two vehicles you can make a twenty-six-kilometer ski-through trip. Follow Penn Boulevard in Silver Bay to the trailhead for the city's Northwoods Ski Trail System. From there you can ski groomed trails to the Tettegouche trailhead, passing through the Palisade Creek valley and Tettegouche Camp along the way. Be sure to start early in the day so that you make it out before dark.

The park has no warming shelters or other facilities. Skiers can use the rest area and headquarters building on Highway 61. When Tettegouche Camp is restored the cabins will be available to skiers. The campground stays open during the winter, but the shower building is closed.

The Palisade Valley Unit

In 1991 Tettegouche State Park nearly doubled in size with the addition of the four-thousand-acre Palisade Valley Unit. Once considered as a possible on-land disposal site for Reserve Mining's taconite tailings, this still-wild area extends to the outskirts of Silver Bay.

Prior to becoming part of Tettegouche State Park, the Palisade area was popular with hunters, snowmobilers, and ATV users. All three activities are still allowed, a rarity in state parks. Local clubs maintain snowmobile trails here and through other portions of Tettegouche.

The Superior Hiking Trail also crosses through the Palisade Valley Unit.

The Shore's best pit stop

The Tettegouche wayside is the only year-round, twenty-four-hour, indoor rest area along the North Shore. Best of all, the wayside stands about midway along the Shore. Nighttime and winter travelers could hardly ask for more.

Is This a Highway or a Portage?

Minnesota Highway 1 between the North Shore and Ely is a sixty mile drive you'll never forget. The scenery is great, but the highway itself leaves the most indelible memories. The stretch north of Isabella must have been a surveyor's nightmare. Meeting the demands of the terrain, the narrow, conifer-shrouded roadway follows a tortuous, serpentine course. You drive this highway at its pace, not yours.

Drive from Finland to Isabella shortly after dawn and you'll likely see a moose. Deer are frequently seen, and coyotes and bears aren't uncommon. Collide with any of them and you might spend the rest of your vacation at a local body shop. Drive carefully.

You can leave the pavement at Finland or Isabella and wander into the Superior National Forest. This area, both inside and outside the Boundary Waters Canoe Area Wilderness, has more lakes than you could fish in a lifetime. Small campgrounds are located at Nine Mile Lake, Little Isabella River, Divide Lake, and Hogback Lake. Outside the wilderness you can pitch a tent most anywhere although some boat accesses are posted with No Camping signs.

The fishing is varied. You can fish for stocked trout in roadside lakes or paddle and portage for walleye. Northern pike as long as your leg swim in some lakes. Most creeks and streams support brook trout, although some waterways north of the divide (in the Hudson's Bay drainage) do not. You can get information about the lakes and streams at the DNR fisheries office in Finland.

Finland

MILEPOST 59+ Don't forget to wear purple if you visit Finland during the St. Urho's Day celebration in March. The good saint is credited with driving the grasshoppers from Finland, and he's remembered annually in mid-March. Finns and would-be Finns, both suffering from cabin fever, turn out in numbers.

Finland has somewhat different roots than other North Shore communities. The first Finnish homesteaders didn't arrive in this remote area until the turn of the century, carrying their possessions on their backs along rough trails leading inland from Lake Superior. They cleared land to farm and lived off wild fish and game. There were no roads, only dogsled trails.

Connections with the outside world improved in the early 1900s as rough roads were built. The first school was built in 1905. (Five children were needed to start a school.) In 1907 the Alger Smith railroad reached the community. The country was rapidly logged off. Large fires raged through the leftover slash in 1908, 1909, and 1910, as well as during the 1920s.

The settlers were mainly farmers. A 1935 government study found 179 Finnish families with a total of 329 acres for hay and 165 acres cleared for crops, including barley, oats, and potatoes. Families grew vegetables in garden plots. Most families had cows, and cream was the only agricultural product that went to market. Officials considered the area poverty stricken, and a state commission recommended that the inhabitants be encouraged to leave. However, others pointed out that Finland residents were better off there than they would be in large cities. The people stayed.

In 1950 the Air Force opened a radar station on a high ridge above Finland. The base, home of the 756th ACWRON Squadron, was expanded during the 1960s, and eighteen homes were built to house personnel. Long-range radar rendered the base obsolete, and it closed in 1980.

Finland remains a quiet community on the Baptism River. Campers can use two nearby riverside campgrounds. The Eckbeck Campground, with thirty primitive sites and a flowing well, is three miles up Highway 1 from Highway 61 along the Baptism River. The Finland Campground, with thirty primitive sites and a pump well is a quarter mile east of Highway 1 on County Road 6 along the East Branch of the Baptism. Both campgrounds are popular on summer weekends and throughout the month of August. Nearby state parks refer overflow campers to these sites.

In "downtown" Finland you'll find a small state forest picnic ground on the banks of the Baptism, with four or five picnic tables, a pump, and an outhouse. All you have to provide is the food.

George Crosby Manitou State Park

MILEPOST 59+ In one North Shore campground you can almost always get a campsite. Of course, there's a catch: you have to carry all your camping gear on your back. George H. Crosby Manitou is Minnesota's only backpacking state park.

Named for George H. Crosby, who donated most of the land, and the Manitou River, which flows through it, the park is reached by driving inland on Highway 1 to Finland and then following Lake County 7 east for seven miles. Day-trippers can picnic on the quiet shores of twenty-acre Benson Lake, which is stocked with trout and has a carry-down boat access. A short hiking trail goes around the lake.

Twenty-three miles of rugged hiking trails traverse the park. Most of the park's twenty-one remote campsites, ranging from a quarter mile to four miles from the parking area, are along the Manitou River. Campers self-register for campsites at the trailhead. Camping reservations are available through Tettegouche State Park.

The river flows through a rugged gorge and over a series of waterfalls. The Cascades are about a mile and a half from the parking area. You can also follow the Superior Hiking Trail from here to Highway 61 at the Caribou River, crossing the Manitou on a new bridge. This section is noted as one of the most scenic areas of the trail.

During the winter the park has no groomed ski trails. The best way to reach the Crosby Manitou backcountry is on a pair of snowshoes. Really adventurous types can ski down the river to Highway 61. However, this excursion is only for those who are very confident of their skiing and winter survival skills as the gorge is very rugged. If you have trouble, it will be a long time before help arrives.

The park has a stand of old-growth yellow birch, which is a designated scientific and natural area. Although most of the park was once logged, you can still see large white pine along the river gorge. These trees generally grow in places that were too difficult to cut. A white pine stump along the Sidewinder hiking trail measures four feet in diameter.

Water, water, everywhere . . .

Visitors are often surprised that good well water is hard to come by in many areas along the North Shore. Crosby Manitou is one such place. The well near the park manager's residence is 155 feet deep and has such low volume during the summer that water must be pumped and stored. A park planning document mentions that some wells in the area have high concentrations of salt.

Can you drink from North Shore streams and lakes? Yes, if you treat or boil the water first. Swimming in some waters is a troublesome parasite called *Giardia lamblia*, from which you can contract a sickness some call beaver fever. This is one nasty bug, and it can turn your insides into an aqueduct. You can purify water using special chemicals or filters or by bringing it to a full boil. Remember, a stream may look fresh and clean, but you can never be sure what lies around the next bend upstream.

MILEPOST 59+ At the Wolf Ridge Environmental Learning Center, the less time kids spend in the classroom, the better. The school has a rule that no more than forty-five minutes of any three-hour class can be spent in the classroom. Rules like that keep learning fun.

So, too, does the subject matter at Wolf Ridge. The goal

Wolf Ridge Environmental Learning Center

of the educational program is to rekindle in students the idea of land stewardship. Classes focus on hands-on experience in ecology, cultural history, and outdoor skills. Students collect maple syrup, learn to snowshoe, collect snow and rain samples to measure acid rain, make canoe paddles, start campfires with flint and steel, band birds, and do a host of other natural activities. Through learning outdoor skills, the students come to understand people's relationship with nature. For many students, this is one of the few opportunities they have to get in the woods.

The school moved to Wolf Ridge, a fourteen-hundred-acre site off Lake County Road 6 between Finland and Little Marais, in 1988 after being in Isabella for eighteen years. The Wolf Ridge Environmental Learning Center is an accredited outdoor school. In a typical week during the school year, the center hosts about two hundred sixth-graders from schools throughout Minnesota. On-site dormitories sleep about 230 people. On weekends and during the summer programs are held for adults and families, including classes for families with preschoolers, a naturalist training program, elderhostel activities, and teacher workshops. About twelve thousand people attend Wolf Ridge programs annually.

Although the school has no activities for people who are just passing through the area, you are welcome to visit and get information about specific programs. The buildings nestle on a high maple ridge where a minimum of clearing was done during construction. The entire facility is heated by a wood-burning unit that consumes about two hundred cords per year.

Brook Trout

If mosquito and blackfly bites were nickels, brook trout anglers would be millionaires. A frying pan full of pink-fleshed brookies doesn't come cheap—you pay blood for them. Few will brave clouds of biting insects and jungles of alder brush to catch fish that measure less than a foot in length. Yet no one else knows the North Shore better than an ardent brook trout angler.

Brook trout are fish of secret places. The best fishing holes are always a long walk from anywhere. You can find them only if you go out and look, because no true angler will show you his or her hot spots. The spirit of the early explorers still lives in brook trout anglers.

Brook trout are native to Lake Superior, but they were not found above the barrier waterfalls that now block steelhead migrations. Superior's brook trout, called coasters, weighed up to five pounds and were caught both in the streams and along the lakeshore. These tremendous trout attracted some of the first tourists to the North Shore. Unfortunately, they couldn't survive changes wrought by humans. They were fished out because they were easy to catch. Log drives destroyed spawning areas, and newly introduced brown and rainbow trout competed for living space. Today coaster brookies are rare.

Brook trout were first stocked in the upper portions of the streams during the early logging days, when milk cans full of fingerlings were dumped from every railroad crossing. They quickly adapted to their new homes, and wild populations developed in every North Shore watershed.

Biologists say that North Shore brookies lead a rigorous life. The streams are infertile and produce a limited amount of aquatic insects and other trout foods. In the summer, many streams nearly dry up, and the water temperatures rise to the upper limits of what brookies can tolerate. During the winter these same streams can freeze to the bottom, trapping trout in the ice.

Still, brook trout survive, although in fewer places than they once did. The state stopped stocking most North Shore streams with brook trout some years ago. In areas where brook trout were unable to successfully reproduce, they have disappeared. Most of the brookies you catch today are wild. So, too, are the places where you fish for them. A typical brook trout stream is small, clear, and shaded by overhanging vegetation. Pools and pockets are rarely more than waist deep. The exception is at beaver dams, where brook trout find both deep water and the food supply they need to grow to larger sizes.

Most North Shore brook trout anglers use worms for bait. It's a Huckleberry Finn kind of sport. You sneak through the brush and dangle your bait in a likely pool. Within moments your fishing rod will telegraph the tap-tap of a bite. You set the hook and lift the wriggling trout from the stream.

Some trout anglers will have nothing to do with worms. Instead they prefer to fool brookies with an artificial fly, preferably one they made. The best time to fly-fish is during June, when mayflies and caddis hatch in the twilight. This is a delicate sport of wandlike fly rods and light leaders. The sight of a fresh-caught brookie is elixir to the soul. Their olive coloration provides a natural camouflage, and their backs are marked with squiggles of lighter green. Along their flanks are small orange spots surrounded with blue halos. The best place to carry the brook trout you catch is on a bed of sweet-smelling ferns in a wicker creel. Dip the creel in the stream occasionally to keep your catch cool and fresh.

A twelve-incher is a trophy in most streams, although a few secluded waters will give up sixteen-inch brutes. You can spend a lifetime looking for such Shangri-las. Is there a better way to enjoy the North Shore?

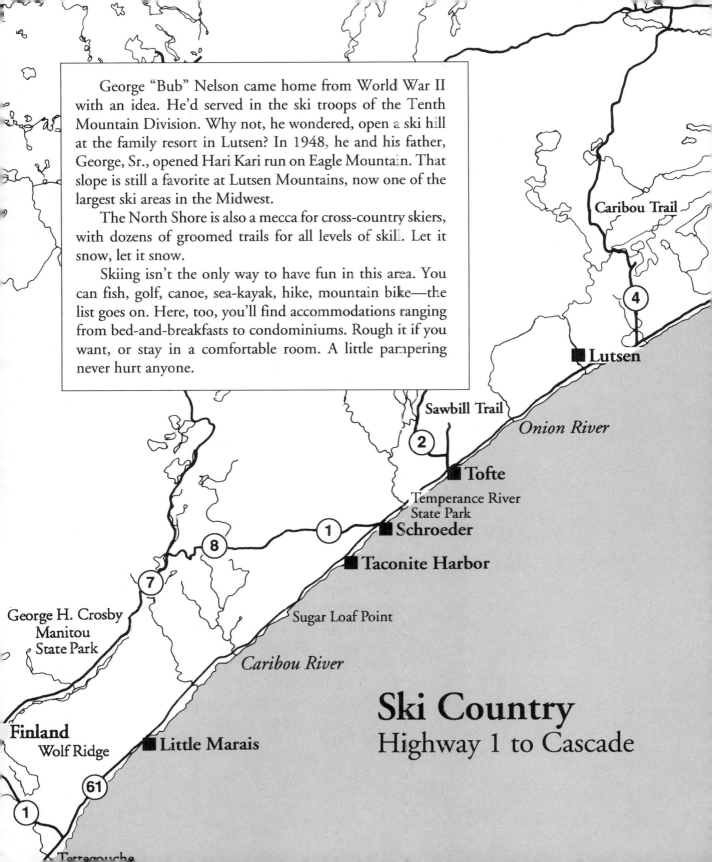

George "Bub" Nelson came home from World War II with an idea. He'd served in the ski troops of the Tenth Mountain Division. Why not, he wondered, open a ski hill at the family resort in Lutsen? In 1948, he and his father, George, Sr., opened Hari Kari run on Eagle Mountain. That slope is still a favorite at Lutsen Mountains, now one of the largest ski areas in the Midwest.

The North Shore is also a mecca for cross-country skiers, with dozens of groomed trails for all levels of skill. Let it snow, let it snow.

Skiing isn't the only way to have fun in this area. You can fish, golf, canoe, sea-kayak, hike, mountain bike—the list goes on. Here, too, you'll find accommodations ranging from bed-and-breakfasts to condominiums. Rough it if you want, or stay in a comfortable room. A little pampering never hurt anyone.

Ski Country
Highway 1 to Cascade

Little Marais

MILEPOST 65 This community has a French name, but a Scandinavian history. Commercial fishermen settled the coastline during the late 1800s. Among those pioneers were Benjamin and Serine Fenstad, whose descendants still live here. The first school was built in 1905, the same year the local post office was established. Telephone service arrived here—and along much of the North Shore—in 1915.

Like other tiny North Shore communities, Little Marais once had more than it does now. Past businesses included a fish company, a gas station, a store, a drive-in, and resorts. The Little Marais Post Office closed in 1980, but you can still find accommodations here. A limited amount of commercial and charter fishing takes place.

Should you write off Little Marais as a do-nothing place? Absolutely not. It is close to other North Shore attractions, and the local lodging establishments offer their guests hiking trails, a boat ramp, and ski trails. Little Marais is a great place to get away from it all.

Caribou River

MILEPOST 70 In the spring it looks so inviting, running dark and clear through the stony riffle above the highway. Unfortunately, steelhead cannot swim this far upstream—they are blocked by a waterfall on private property below. The parking lot at the Caribou is not for anglers, but for hikers. Upstream about a half mile is one of the most spectacular waterfalls along the shore.

This area is known as Caribou Falls State Park, but it has no facilities other than outdoor privies. The trail to the falls, even though recently improved, is still slick and muddy after it rains. Take that as a word of caution, though, not as advice to avoid the trail. The sight of the rain-swollen Caribou roaring off the cliff is unforgettable.

The trail follows closely beside the stream, which tumbles

and glides beneath a canopy of birch and cedar. Walk quietly, keep a keen eye on the hillside, and you may see a deer, especially in winter or spring. Look for their tracks in muddy portions of the trail. Along the river you may find the tracks of other animals, such as mink. The river is called "Caribou," but caribou disappeared in this watershed at least one hundred years ago.

At the falls the trail gets a bit treacherous. You can climb over a rock ridge and then descend to the falls on a steep loose-rock trail. When you reach the river you're so close it's difficult to photograph the falls. You'll have to get wet for the best shots, but wading the Caribou in high water certainly isn't recommended. Ditto for walking on ice, especially in the spring.

The falls trail links with the Superior Hiking Trail. Walk west toward Crosby Manitou State Park, or hike east and you'll come out on Lake County 1 near Dyers Lake, where the Two Island River crosses.

The Superior Hiking Trail

Mountain folk may scoff at these hills, but the North Shore's rocky spine with its sawtooth peaks is about as rugged as it gets in the Midwest. In fact, the view from the top is distinctly un-Midwestern. From the maple ridges you look out upon the queen of inland seas. Sometimes you can see hawks soaring below you.

Until recently, only deer hunters, berry pickers, and a few adventurous souls who wandered the hillsides knew many of the vistas and quiet places on those ridges. Now you can follow the North Shore ridges and explore valleys and canyons for 160 miles along the Superior Hiking Trail. Aside from a gap near Little Marais, the trail follows a continuous course from Castle Danger to Kadunce Creek. Plans are to complete the trail to the Canadian border.

The trail is being constructed with state funding, but volunteer groups will adopt and maintain sections of the trail. Building the trail has been no small undertaking. First a route taking advantage of both scenery and terrain was planned. Then trail easements were acquired from landowners. Finally, a route was marked with plastic flagging and trail crews got to work.

The resulting footpath has log steps and half-log planking where necessary. Sturdy bridges span creeks and rivers—some are such marvels of engineering that they appear incongruous in their remote setting. Hike at your own pace; a person in average physical condition will do just fine.

Roads cross the trail at five- to ten-mile intervals. This means hikers get the advantages of two worlds. Day hikers can plan short but wild trips. Backpackers can choose terrific multiday hikes, an uncommon hiking option in the Midwest. In western Cook County lodge-to-lodge hiking is available.

As with all North Shore trails, the Superior Hiking Trail has lots of ups and downs. Aside from a planned stretch along the cobblestone beach between Kadunce Creek and Judge C. R. Magney State Park, or an occasional dip into a river valley like Devil Track Canyon, the trail follows the ridgeline five hundred feet above the lake.

Which stretch is the best? None of the trail is dull, but some sections are more popular than others. The huffing and puffing it takes to reach the top of Carlton Peak above Tofte, over a mile from the road, is rewarded by the view. So too is a walk in the opposite direction from the Sawbill Trail to the top of Britton Peak, a mile round trip. Further east, off Forest Road 336, trudging the Oberg Mountain loop is a "must" for many September leaf lookers.

If you have a taste for the high, wide, and lonesome, try the ten-mile section between Penn Boulevard in Silver Bay and Tettegouche State Park. The terrain is surprisingly mountainous. A boulder field extending into its clear waters gives Bean Lake an alpine appearance. Yes, there are trout here. There are also trout in every stream the trail crosses, although fishing in some is disappointing. The DNR stocks many streams with steelhead fry, which grow up to be tiny rainbow trout before they get the urge to migrate to Lake Superior. You'll have fast action with the half-pint rainbows, but brook trout—the prize of stream anglers—are scarce.

What is the best hiking season? Fall is certainly most colorful; the weather is cool and mosquitos few. In early spring waterfalls roar with meltwater. Mosquitos and blackflies can be a problem during the summer, but those willing to brave the bugs can treat themselves to handfuls of strawberries, blueberries, and raspberries. Winter snowshoers have little company other than ravens, wolves, and chickadees. The Superior Hiking trail is ready when you are.

Becoming trailwise

The beauty of hiking is its simplicity. You don't need to take out a second mortgage on the house to outfit the family with gear. All you really need is a comfortable pair of shoes or boots that you don't mind getting dirty. Nonslip soles are preferable, because wet rocks and muddy spots can be slick.

If you plan to hike for an hour or more, be sure to carry a supply of water. Generations of outdoor enthusiasts have drunk water from North Shore streams, but experts advise against this practice. *Giardia* is present in some waters. Treat or boil stream water to be safe.

During the warm months, especially June and July, don't forget the bug repellent. Phenomenal numbers of mosquitos and blackflies can make short work of unprotected hikers. However, if you wear repellent, they'll generally leave you alone.

Of course, a good map is essential to any hike. You are unlikely to get hopelessly lost in this country, but you could become confused. In many areas the hiking trail intersects ski trails, snowmobile routes, and old logging roads. Signs have been installed to mark the Superior Hiking Trail, but an appalling number of hikers tear them down to bring home as souvenirs. The official trail map shows some, but not all, of the intersecting trails. Hikers should carry a compass and know how to use it.

Campsites are also marked on the trail map and are available on a first-come, first-served basis. Campsites have a fire ring, tent pad, and pit toilet. You may camp just about anywhere along the trail unless the land is posted as private.

The trail receives routine maintenance, but don't be surprised to see windfalls, especially after storms. Usually it is safer to go around a windfall than to climb over it.

Wildlife

Lucky hikers may see more animals than people on the Superior Hiking Trail, especially if they walk quietly. Humans are usually the noisiest creatures in the North Woods, shouting, singing, talking, and laughing. All that commotion scares wildlife away. Look and listen instead of talking when you are in the woods. You'll be rewarded with close-up views of wild animals.

What are you likely to see? The most common creatures are red squirrels, chipmunks, ruffed grouse, and songbirds. Quiet hikers are likely to see white-tailed deer and, in some areas, moose. Try to avoid close encounters with moose, especially during the fall when they are in rut. Never argue with these cantankerous critters.

Some people are afraid of meeting bears and wolves when they head into the forest. That fear is largely unfounded. Both animals are so shy that even seeing one is uncommon. And if you do, you usually get no more than a quick glimpse as it makes a fast exit.

Walk the trail during the evening and you may hear owls, coyotes, or even timber-wolves. Several species of raptors, including peregrine falcons, live in these lonely hills. During the fall the North Shore is a major migration route for hawks, vultures, and eagles. You also may see flocks of Canada, blue, and snow geese passing far overhead. Other animals that may cross your path include pine marten, mink, and fisher.

What about Lyme disease?

Should North Shore hikers be worried about Lyme disease? Yes, as well as lightning strikes, moose attacks, and falling trees. This is not to belittle the hazard of Lyme disease, but to put it into perspective. The illness has been reported on the North Shore, but it is by no means epidemic. One health official said you have far more risk of being murdered during a two-day stay in Chicago than you have of contracting Lyme disease during a two-day hike on the North Shore. However, an ounce of prevention is worth a pound of cure.

Lyme disease is transmitted to humans by the bite of the deer tick, a tiny cousin of the common wood tick. A close inspection of the two reveals identifying differences. Deer ticks have a black, pointed head shaped like a sharp pencil, and a reddish body. Wood ticks have a dull, blunt head and whitish markings on the body. Wood ticks are twice as large as deer ticks.

The percentage of deer ticks infected with Lyme disease varies from place to place and year to year. Adult deer ticks prefer deer as a food source. However, deer ticks in the nymphal stage will attach themselves to any warm-blooded animal that passes by. You are most likely to contract Lyme disease from the nymph.

Humans are not the only animals that contract Lyme disease. Infected white-tailed deer show no symptoms. The largest reservoir of the disease is in rodents and ground birds. It has also been diagnosed in pets, and a vaccine exists for them. Although you cannot get Lyme disease from an animal bite, you might be at risk if an open wound is exposed to the blood of an infected animal.

Deer ticks can be found anywhere, and are even brought indoors by humans and pets. If the air temperature is above freezing, they're out and about. However, the highest risk of being bitten occurs during the summer when you are wearing less clothing.

The best way to avoid Lyme disease is by making your body an inhospitable place for ticks. Occasionally brush off your clothing when outdoors. DEET-based insect repellants will discourage but not kill ticks. Permanone, available in outdoor shops, kills ticks, and you can use it on clothing.

Examine yourself for ticks when bathing or showering. Biting deer ticks can be removed with a good pair of tweezers. Don't panic if you are bitten, but do look for symptoms that may occur during the next few weeks.

The most distinctive symptom of Lyme disease is a ringlike rash that appears within a month of the bite. The rash may be accompanied by fever, chills, and swollen lymph nodes. If unchecked, symptoms may expand to include fatigue, muscle and joint pain, facial palsy, weakness, and an irregular heartbeat. Individuals may experience a variety of symptoms, and the disease may even resemble another illness. Blood tests are used for Lyme disease diagnosis, but they are not completely reliable.

If untreated, Lyme disease can knock you for a loop. Many cases develop into arthritis attacks of large joints, especially the knee. Some individuals suffer chronic problems in the skin, joints, or nervous system.

If diagnosed at an early stage, Lyme disease can be treated with oral antibiotics. If the disease has progressed to later stages, intravenous antibiotics may be required.

Staying out of trouble

Accidents do happen on the North Shore. Emergency workers can tell you all sorts of stories, including some with unhappy endings. In the woods, even a minor accident can become a major emergency.

The smart backcountry explorer is prepared for trouble. Always tell someone where you're going before you leave. If you do have trouble and don't return on time, they'll know where to start looking for you. Carry a map and compass, and know how to use both.

Common sense will keep you out of trouble. Don't do foolish things like playing near the edge of cliffs, swimming in flood-swollen streams, or feeding bears and other wild animals. Be careful when you're using hatchets and hunting knives. Wear clothing that is appropriate for the country and the climate—even if you plan to spend most of the time in your car.

If the worst does happen, there are hospitals in Duluth, Two Harbors, and Grand Marais. Every community has trained emergency workers, both volunteer and professional. You'll be in good hands.

Sugar Loaf Landing

MILEPOST 73 You may not find Sugar Loaf Landing unless you know where to look. The gravel drive that leads from the highway to the lake is unmarked and blocked with a gate. In the winter, you can see the Sugar Loaf rock formation through the leafless trees as you approach along the highway from the east. The land was once owned by Consolidated Papers of Wisconsin Rapids. From 1943 to 1971 the company used the site to build immense rafts of pulpwood, which were towed to Ashland, Wisconsin. From there the logs went by rail to the company's pulp and paper mills. The company had several buildings on the beach at Sugar Loaf, but all were destroyed by wave action.

This little-known beach may well become an environmental battlefield. The land at Sugar Loaf is now owned by the state, which acquired it from the Nature Conservancy. The site has been named as a potential location for a publicly funded harbor of refuge. The multimillion-dollar project would enclose a water basin of about ten acres and might also be linked to some sort of commercial development. Not everyone thinks that's a good idea.

Sugar Loaf is but one of several environmental conflicts along the North Shore. The root of each issue is usually the same: as increasing numbers of people discover the North Shore, they exert growing pressure to develop new and larger facilities. Economic and social gains must be weighed against environmental loss. It will be up to future generations to decide if we made the right decisions.

Taconite Harbor

MILEPOST 77 The size of a modern ore carrier is almost beyond a landlubber's comprehension. These one-thousand-foot behemoths—longer than three football fields—can carry sixty thousand tons of taconite pellets in their holds. From the observation area on the west side of LTV Mining's Taconite Harbor facility, you can watch these mighty ships take on a load.

Taconite Harbor was constructed during the 1950s as a port for mining operations at Hoyt Lakes. The mines and the harbor are connected by a seventy-four-mile railroad. Trains average ninety-six cars, which are each equipped with automatic dumping apparatus. It takes only fifteen minutes for a train to unload at the dock.

A 2,334-foot pier protects the harbor. The dock where the boats load is 1,200 feet long and contains twenty-five ore bins. Each bin has a shuttle conveyor for loading the ships. With the efficient computerized operation, a one-thousand-foot carrier can be loaded in four hours. About 7.5 million tons of taconite are shipped from the port annually.

The harbor also has a coal dock. Ships deliver coal here to fuel LTV's power plant. The facility has three seventy-five-megawatt boiler turbine generator units. The plant went on line in 1957 and operated until a 1982 shutdown. It was restarted in 1991.

LTV employs about 1,650 people, 75 of whom work at Taconite Harbor. A small "company town" once stood on the west side of the site, but the homes were moved in 1990.

Father Baraga's Landfall

MILEPOST 79 In August 1843, the Reverend F. R. Baraga, a Catholic missionary, set out in a small craft from the Indian village of La Pointe on Wisconsin's Madeline Island. Somewhere during the thirty-plus-mile voyage he and his paddlers were overtaken by a storm.

Anyone who has ventured onto Lake Superior in a small craft knows how vulnerable you feel when the waves begin cresting into whitecaps. Today we have outboard motors and boat landings. Father Baraga and his companions used only their strength and wits to battle the angry seas. The powerful waves could have easily shattered their small craft or washed someone overboard.

Eventually, Baraga landed safely near a river mouth. There he nailed a wooden cross to a tall stump. On the cross he inscribed "In commemoration of the goodness of Almighty God in granting to the Reverend F. R. Baraga, Missionary, a safe traverse from La Pointe to this place, August, 1843."

Today a small sign on Highway 61 reads "Father Baraga's Cross." A short paved road leads to a small parking lot at the mouth of the Cross River, where a concrete cross marks the missionary's voyage. The area has neither picnic tables nor toilets, but the ledgerock shoreline is a pleasant place for a picnic. A small but serviceable ramp allows you to launch a small boat, and if you're lucky, you may see an ore carrier enter nearby Taconite Harbor.

The small community through which the Cross River flows is called Schroeder, in memory of a logging company president. Around the turn of the century tall pine was cut here, driven down the rivers, and then rafted across the lake. The community's first settlers, the Henry Redmyer family, were fishermen and sailors who established a homestead on the west bank of the river during the 1880s.

The logging years were Schroeder's liveliest era. Hundreds of loggers worked felling white pine. Two saloons and a bordello in Schroeder gave them an outlet for their spare time and money. Certainly, these operations boosted the local economy—lumberjacks had no need to travel to Duluth.

Now Schroeder is better known for good, clean fun. The Schroeder Town Hall, the largest community gathering place in western Cook County, throughout the year is the scene of folk music concerts sponsored by the North Shore Music Association. Occasionally the acts are local—many fine folk musicians live in the surrounding area; or the entertainers may come from the Twin Cities and beyond. If you enjoy folk music, inquire locally to find out if any concerts are planned.

Schroeder also hosts a continuous natural concert—the sound of the Cross River plunging over the waterfalls at the Highway 61 bridge. This waterfall is the most accessible on the North Shore, because you don't need to leave your vehicle to see it. However, a parking lot on the west side of the river and a walkway at the bridge allow you to get an even closer view. Be careful. This is not a place to test your rock climbing skills. The Cross River is as unforgiving as it is beautiful.

Smuggler's roost?

A century ago, opium was a common ingredient in many patent medicines. Although legal, the drug was subject to high tariffs, so smugglers found a ready market.

In 1894, federal agents, suspicious of the fishermen who plied Lake Superior waters, began an investigation. A few weeks later they seized Henry Redmyer's schooner, *Emilie,* in Two Harbors. The schooner was hauled to Duluth and thoroughly searched, but no contraband was found.

The federal government still searches for drug smugglers on Lake Superior. The United States Border Patrol has a cigarette boat used to investigate anglers and sailors. The cigarette boat, a comparative rarity on Lake Superior, is often docked at the Coast Guard station in Grand Marais.

Temperance River State Park

MILEPOST 80 The Temperance River received its name from early travelers because there was no "bar" at its mouth. They could easily bring a fair-sized craft into the lagoon and camp on the sloping west bank of the river. This natural harbor of refuge continued to be used by boaters until the late 1970s when the river flooded following a terrible rainstorm. Large quantities of gravel washed down the river and collected at the mouth. Now a gravel bar nearly blocks the channel during the winter. Spring runoff pushes the gravel out into the lake, but wave action throughout the summer and fall gradually pushes it back into the river. A shifting, gravel beach now exists on the lakeshore near the river mouth.

Camping remains popular. Back when the highway was no more than a rutted trail, campers pitched tents west of the river. Now a fifty-site campground is located on the east side. Throughout summer and fall the No Vacancy sign hangs at the campground access every night. As in all state parks, 70 percent of the sites can be reserved in advance. The other 30 percent are available on a first-come, first-served basis. The campground has no hookups, but showers are available.

Why is this campground so popular? One reason is that it within an easy day's drive of every North Shore attraction, from Duluth to Thunder Bay. Another is the park's beauty. The Temperance River slices through narrow gorges. The Ojibwa name, *Kawimbash,* meant "Deep Hollow River." The gorges were formed as swirling water carried sand and gravel across the soft lava flows, digging "potholes" in the rock, depressions that eventually connected to make the gorge. The process continues. Along the bank you can see potholes that were left behind when the river shifted course.

On warm summer days pools in the river look particularly inviting. Swimming is allowed at your own risk, except in areas marked with No Swimming signs. However, river swimmers *anywhere* on the Shore must put safety first. A pool beneath a waterfall may be an exciting place when the water is low, but a deadly maelstrom at higher levels. North Shore rivers rise rapidly after summer rains. If you're unfamiliar with a river be especially cautious. Drownings have occurred in the Temperance and other streams.

Anglers will find plenty to catch in the Temperance, although the river is difficult to fish. Lakerun trout and salmon can swim only a short distance upstream from the lagoon. Farther upstream you can find brook and brown trout, but rugged terrain and fast water make for tough access. If you don't want to work hard for your fish, try shore-casting near the river mouth. Lake trout are commonly taken after the spring smelt run, as well as throughout summer and fall. In recent years smelting success has varied each spring. Chinook salmon once made heavy September runs, but salmon stocking has been discontinued in the Temperance.

Hiking trails follow both river banks. The Superior Hiking Trail crosses the Temperance about a mile upstream, so you can make a scenic loop trip. More ambitious hikers can follow the Superior Hiking Trail across Carlton Peak and have someone meet them at the parking lot on the Sawbill Trail. Several routes head west to the Cross River and more than twenty-five hundred acres of undeveloped state land.

In the winter these trails are groomed for cross-country skiing. Temperance State Park trails also link with the Tofte-Lutsen trail system. The Temperance River Trail, which is moderately difficult to ski, has exceptional scenery. The Upper Cross River Trail offers a more leisurely route. All trails are well-marked, but accurate maps are locally available. Skiers can park on Highway 61.

Hikers and skiers will enjoy the striking beauty of the prominent birch hillsides. Unlike many areas along the Shore, the forest here looks much as it did before the coming of Europeans. One significant change is that white-tailed deer now heavily browse the area. You can see signs of deer in the park throughout the year. In the winter, skiers should watch for timber-wolf tracks.

Brr!

Heatwaves are rare at Temperance River State Park. Climate information in park records reveals the following chilly facts. The temperature falls below zero an average of fifty-five days per year. In an average year, the mercury never climbs above ninety degrees. The park receives twenty-eight inches of precipitation annually, including sixty-five to seventy inches of snow. The lakeshore is not only cool, but windy. Prevailing northeast winds exceed thirty miles an hour on an average of thirty days from May through September.

MILEPOST 82 People named Tofte still live in the village of Tofte. The community is not named for them, but for an island village in Norway, birthplace of settlers Hans and Torger Engelsen and twin brothers John and Andrew Tofte—Toftevaag. The Norwegians arrived in 1893, claiming abandoned homesteads. Fishermen, farmers, and loggers, they carved out homes in the wilderness.

Looming above Tofte is Carlton Peak, one of the few North Shore "mountains" visible from Highway 61. Minnesota Mining and Manufacturing has owned it since 1903— it may have been the first property 3M purchased. The company intended to quarry corundum to make grinding wheels, but the enterprise never worked out. However, the state highway department occasionally uses the distinctive rock quarried from Carlton Peak when rock is needed for highway work. It can be seen in the breakwalls at Taconite Harbor and Grand Marais. You can hike to the peak from a Superior Hiking Trail parking lot along the Sawbill Trail north of Tofte.

Tofte

Today the community's economy is based upon tourism and logging. The Bluefin Bay resort complex occupies the shoreline where "herring chokers" once dried their nets. On the west side of Tofte, a United States Forest Service office provides information about the Superior National Forest and BWCAW. Adjacent to the ranger station is Birch Grove Center, a focal point for the community. In the mid 1980s, when enrollment declined and tight budgets forced the closing of Birch Grove Elementary School, residents banded together to form the Birch Grove Foundation. Now the community and Cook County school district jointly operate the small school. In order to keep costs down, space in the building is leased to small businesses. The unusual arrangement works, and shows how tiny North Shore communities pool resources in order to provide needed services.

A boat launching area and picnic grounds lie west of Bluefin Bay. The launching area has a small dock, but little protection from lake winds, so boaters should pay close attention to the weather. The picnic area is the site of Tofte's locally famous Fourth of July celebration. Visitors on the Fourth can expect a full day of fun activities and an evening fireworks display.

A Piece of the Rock

The North Shore has a varied real estate market. In places like Silver Bay, home prices have yet to recover from the Reserve Mining closure, yet in others, like Lutsen, Lake Superior frontage costs $400 to $600 a foot. Potential buyers often spend a long time looking for the place they want at a price they can afford. Very little property is actually available. Only about 10 percent of Cook County, for instance, is privately owned.

Most prime Lake Superior shoreline is already developed, although east of Grand Marais some undeveloped shoreline is still available. Recently, the hottest selling properties have been those without lake frontage but with a view of the lake, as prices are much lower. Building on the North Shore requires special considerations. In some areas good well water is difficult to find. Builders must often contend with rock outcrops and difficult terrain. Consequently, installing a septic system is expensive. Power is not available in some inland areas and the road past your retreat may not be plowed during the winter. However, none of this deters those who have fallen in love with the Shore and feel they must have a piece of it for their very own.

Real estate values have risen rapidly in recent years, but land prices here are still downright cheap compared to other parts of the country. "Outsiders" are often willing to plunk down amounts of money that surprise even high-rolling Midwesterners. If you're in the market for North Shore property, do some research prior to parting with your hard-earned cash. Local real estate agents can provide a wealth of information. So, too, can persons who have already purchased their North Shore hideaway. A visit to the county assessor's office is in order as well. Well-informed buyers make smart purchases.

Winter Driving

Highway 61 is well-plowed by state highway crews during the snowy months, but snowstorm driving is never fun. Along the Shore you can see snow anytime from October to May, with a few pavement-polishing freezing rains tossed in to keep things interesting. Weather forecasts are often laughably inaccurate, so wintertime travelers should be prepared. Never travel without proper winter clothing, which includes a warm coat, hat, mittens or gloves, and winter boots.

Drive very slowly when it is raining or snowing. Highway 61 is narrow, bumpy, and rarely straight, so you have little room for recovery if you begin to slide. Heavy snowfalls can reduce visibility to zero. Don't assume that deer and other animals are bedded down to wait out the storm. The moment you relax you'll see one standing in the road.

The John Beargrease Sled Dog Races

The North Shore is cruelly beautiful in January. On subzero nights the trees crack as loudly as rifle shots. At dawn the lake lies smothered beneath cold mists. The hard-packed snow squeaks when you walk on it. You might say January is a time fit for neither man nor beast, but you'd be wrong. For mushers and their sled dogs, January is the best time of year.

Sled dogs have a long history on the North Shore. For centuries they were the rapid transit system of the North, an efficient means of winter travel. During the first decades of white settlement along the North Shore, mushers and their teams provided the only link with the outside world, as men and dogs hauled mail up the Shore along a rugged trail.

One of the mushing mailmen was an Ojibwa named John Beargrease. He lived in Beaver Bay with his wife, Louisa, and their children and delivered mail from Two Harbors to Grand Marais on a weekly basis during the late 1800s. In the warm months he rowed and sailed a small boat. When the snow fell he used four dogs to pull a mail sled weighing four hundred to seven hundred pounds. The dogs wore bells on their collars to frighten away wolves. The jingle of those bells was a welcome sound indeed at the isolated homesteads and communities along the Shore. Beargrease delivered mail until 1899, when the completion of the Old North Shore Road allowed mail to be carried on a horse-drawn stage.

Sled dogs lost their prominence as winter transportation improved, but trappers and others who traveled the backcountry still used them. During the 1970s interest in recreational mushing grew, and a number of North Shore residents kept small teams. Sprint races were held to determine who had the fastest dogs. Eventually a longer race evolved, and the first Gunflint Mailrun was held at Gunflint Lake in 1977. The next year the race began in downtown Grand Marais and followed snowmobile trails to Hungry Jack Lodge off the Gunflint Trail.

The Mailrun was an annual event until 1980, when WDSM Radio in Duluth sponsored a race from Grand Marais to Duluth. In 1984 the race, now called the John Beargrease Sled Dog Race, was lengthened to a marathon distance, with mushers going from Duluth to Grand Marais and back. In 1988 the race route was extended to Grand Portage, for a round-trip distance of nearly five hundred miles. That year the Beargrease 130, a middle-distance race from Grand Marais to Two Harbors, began. That race proved so popular that in 1990 another short race, the Beargrease 90 from Grand Marais to Beaver Bay, was added to the lineup.

In the early years the Beargrease was essentially a local phenomenon, with Minnesota mushers such as Kevin Turnbough, John Patten, and Robin Jacobson being the first across the finish line. However, when the Beargrease grew in stature and started offering larger purses, it attracted more attention from the mushing world. Alaskan mushers, veterans of the Iditarod, came south to give the Lower 48 mushers a run for the money. Mushing megastars such as Susan Butcher and Dee Dee Jonrowe have since chalked up Beargrease wins.

Marathon mushing attracts a different sort of spectator. Like the mushers, race watchers are a special breed. The only place where you can sit in the bleachers and cheer dogs and drivers is at Duluth's Ordean Field where the race begins. The racers quickly enter the woods, emerging from the trees only at road crossings and checkpoints. Serious spectators intercept them at these points, huddling beside campfires to catch a glimpse of the teams as they pass by. The marathon lasts five days or more, and teams spread out along the trail. Spectators often choose to follow one or two favorite teams.

This is one of the few sports where spectators can become participants. When a team arrives at a lonely checkpoint everyone pitches in to help out. You may find yourself stepping from the sidelines to help hold a team while the musher checks in. The road crossings and checkpoints are staffed by a dedicated cadre of volunteers willing to brave anything from double-digit subzero temperatures to blizzards for the good of the race. Many sit through long nights waiting for the racers to come in, often with no more protection from the elements than a tent or the cab of a pickup truck.

You cannot spend much time around mushers without developing a deep respect for their dogs. Sled dogs are athletes that undergo months of training and conditioning prior to racing. They are born to pull, and their excited yips and howls prior to a run are proof of their love for racing. In fact, a dog team's competitive spirit can win races. Rare is the musher who will mistreat dogs; most give their teams topflight care, including special diets, regular workouts, and veterinary attention. A dog's life indeed!

Dogspeak

Like any sport, mushing has buzzwords and special terms. Hang around a checkpoint and you'll quickly learn the language. For instance, when a team is ready to run the musher calls, "Hike! Hike!"—not "Mush! Mush!"—to get the dogs started. The command "Gee!" tells the dogs to turn right, while "Haw!" means turn left. "Whoa!" means stop.

Long-distance racing teams consist of a dozen or more dogs harnessed in pairs to a gangline. At the front of the team the lead dog takes the commands and sets the pace. Behind it are a pair known as the point dogs, followed by a pair called the swing dogs. Directly in front of the sled are the wheel dogs. Depending upon snow conditions, the team may wear booties to protect their feet.

The driver stands on runners extending from the back of the sled. The cargo area of the sled is called the basket. Early in the race a driver may carry a passenger in order to curb an exuberant team. Otherwise, the basket is used to carry food and water needed on the trail, or to transport an injured dog.

When a team is "parked," the sled may be tied down with a snub line or held in place with an anchor called a snow hook.

Watching the race

Because the races follow woodland trails, the only places where you can see the teams are at the start, the checkpoints, and the finish line. This means it's essential to be in the right place at the right time. You can get race updates at the checkpoints and from local radio reports.

If you crave action, you'll find the best spectating at the start lines. The marathon begins on a midweek evening from Ordean Field in Duluth. The teams leave singly at intervals. A similar procedure is used for the 130 and 90, which start from Coast Guard Point in Grand Marais on Saturday afternoon. Here onlookers have a chance to mingle with the mushers prior to the races. Most middle-distance racers are hobbyists who love the sport or up-and-coming marathoners who are still building their teams. As a rule, they're knowledgeable and friendly.

At the checkpoints, moments of excitement interrupt hours of waiting. At the Idle Hour, Skyport, Grand Portage, and Tofte, you can wait in the warmth of a restaurant or bar. However, the most interesting checkpoint is the Sawbill Trail, which the teams reach on the second day of the race. This is where many mushers elect to take their mandatory twelve-hour layover so there's usually lots of action with teams coming and going. You can swap stories around campfires, drink coffee, and munch on hot dogs provided by local volunteers. For the 130 and the 90 races, the Pike Lake checkpoint gets the nod.

The Sawbill Trail

MILEPOST 82 The Sawbill Trail climbs north from Tofte into the Superior National Forest. The initial six miles are paved, and the asphalt would extend further into the forest if zealous local planners had their way. Instead, concerned citizens teamed up to derail pavement plans. The rest of the Sawbill remains a gravel "trail."

The Sawbill follows the Temperance River valley for miles. The Temperance, one of the largest North Shore rivers, originates in a chain of BWCAW lakes. Interestingly, one of the river's sources, Brule Lake, also feeds the mighty Brule River, which enters Lake Superior about fifty miles farther up the Shore. Two riverside campgrounds provide a stopping place along the Trail.

Several gravel side roads intersect with the Sawbill. The first, the Old 600 Road (Forest Road #166), heads west at the end of the pavement. At the intersection you can still find foundations from a CCC camp. In the winter this is the site of the Sawbill checkpoint for the John Beargrease Sled Dog Marathon. Hospitality shines at what locals call "the only wilderness checkpoint."

You can follow #166 westward all the way to Highway 1. Beyond the Temperance it crosses what is known as Heartbreak Hill. Two explanations exist for the hill's name: that the hill was a heartbreaker for teams of horses hauling logs, and that a pioneer lost his family to tuberculosis here.

The next side road is the Honeymoon Trail, which heads east to the Caribou Trail. Following this route you'll return to Highway 61 at Lutsen. The Honeymoon got its name when the area's first Superior National Forest ranger, John Mulligan, walked across it with his new bride on their way to the Four Mile Lake Ranger Station. Lakes to the north bear the name of his wife, Grace, and their daughters. Shrouded by sugar maples, the Honeymoon is breathtaking in September.

Beyond the Honeymoon the Sawbill traverses a series of

pine-covered eskers, glacial gravel deposits. Much of this area burned during a 1948 forest fire.

The next road to cross the Sawbill is built upon the old Alger-Smith Railroad grade. Not many years ago you could still bounce over the railroad ties. The line extended all the way to Rose Lake on the Canadian border. The present gravel thoroughfare goes east to Devil Track Lake. Along the way you'll pass Gust Lake, which was the home of an early bootlegger. Near Cascade Lake stand the remains of a logging town called Cascade. The forest has reclaimed the site, but you can still find it from the road. Ask for specific directions at the Tofte Ranger Station.

To the west this gravel road connects with a network of forest roads. Using a Superior National Forest map you can find your way to the old Wanless homestead at Harriet Lake. Settlers once inhabited this area, but their clearings are now overgrown. The Forest Service maintains the opening at the Wanless homestead for species such as bluebirds. This is an excellent bird watching area, and during the summer the roses that once brightened the homestead still bloom. Both directions on "The Grade" (Forest Roads #170 and #165) are good early-morning bets for moose watching. However, be careful. This broad roadway encourages drivers to drive too fast.

The Sawbill Trail ends at Sawbill Lake on the edge of the BWCAW. From here you can paddle all the way to the Canadian border and beyond without crossing another road. If such a wilderness journey is a larger bite than you care to chew, try a day trip on Sawbill Lake, the Kelso River, and Alton Lake, an easy route where you'll see few people. Outfitters in Tofte and at Sawbill Lake rent canoes.

Oh yes, the fishing. Many lakes in the Sawbill country are excellent walleye producers. As a rule, dusk brings the best walleye fishing. You don't need the latest in tackle and technology to catch your share of fish. Try jigs, floaters, or slip bobber rigs baited with minnows or leeches. Move around until you locate an active school of fish. Then catching enough for dinner shouldn't be difficult. You may also catch northern pike or smallmouth bass.

Fall color routes

In mid-September the sugar maple ridges of the Sawtooth Mountains blaze with scarlet and orange. An area off the Cramer Road above Schroeder is an old-growth research site for the United States Forest Service. Another site near Agnes Lake off the Caribou Trail is also being considered for research. These forests are predominately maple; but other species, such as the uncommon yellow birch, grow there, too.

Leaf looking has become an immensely popular autumn activity. The best time to see maples is in the latter half of September. Aspen and birch, both yellow, peak along the lakeshore in October, making the fall color season nearly a month in length. Tofte is a good place to begin a fall foliage excursion, because the Forest Service has marked several driving routes, which are accessible from Highway 61 and the Sawbill Trail. In some places, such as along Forest Road #166 and the Honeymoon Trail, you'll drive beneath maple canopies. Just north of Tofte along the Sawbill Trail a short but steep path leads to the top of Britton Peak, where you'll find a panoramic view of Carlton Peak, Tofte, and Lake Superior.

Fall colors along the North Shore are stunning. This is no secret, so make reservations far in advance no matter where you plan to stay along the Shore. On autumn weekends it is not uncommon for all accommodations to be filled between Hinckley and Thunder Bay!

You can also obtain fall color tour maps for the Tofte-Lutsen area. Signs mark most routes, and some extra-rough roads—not included on the recommended tours—are marked with warning signs.

Thirsty?

During the 1930s, CCC crews on the Sawbill needed a water supply. They found one five miles up the Sawbill Trail. The spring, encased in a water pipe, is on the right side of the trail about a mile before the intersection with Forest Road #166.

Half of the fun of exploring backcountry roads is happening upon wildlife. For many, the sight of a moose, loon, or osprey can make the trip. The Forest Service recommends the Grade (Forest Road 165) as a good place to look for northern wildlife. The stretch between the Sawbill and Caribou trails crosses and recrosses the Temperance River and then weaves between several lakes.

Because many northern animals live near water, this diverse and swampy habitat makes for good viewing. Look for moose, beavers, and otters, as well as loons, osprey, common mergansers, and black ducks. Stop at river crossings and beside lakes and get out of your vehicle for a closer look. You are most likely to see wildlife at dawn and dusk.

Watchable Wildlife

The ruffed grouse

Hike a North Shore trail on a pleasant spring day and you may hear a strange sound emanating from the forest. Those unfamiliar with the noise say it sounds like someone trying to start a one-lung gasoline engine that sputters to life and then stops. Those more savvy in the ways of the woods will immediately recognize the drumming of the male ruffed grouse.

The ruffed grouse mating ritual is as old as the forest. Each spring, soon after the snow melts, the male stands upon the "drumming log" that is the focal point of his territory. He leans back upon his fanned-out tail and begins beating his wings against the air with an increasing tempo. A momentary vacuum created by the rapid wingbeats causes the drumming sound. The listener hears a thumping sound that lasts for several seconds, reaching a crescendo and then fading. Although grouse drum throughout the year, they are most frequently heard during the spring breeding season.

The purpose of all this noise is to attract a female. When one appears, the male goes into a splendid display. He fans his tail, with its distinctive dark band near the tips of the feathers. The dark, iridescent ruff on his neck is erect and full. He struts about, holding his wings so the tips touch the ground. Few grouse hens can resist such a Romeo.

Although many people hear drumming grouse, few actually see the bird in action. Spring trout anglers are attending to other business, and careless hikers frighten the birds as they approach. However, if you are patient and stealthy, you can observe drumming grouse. The trick is to listen carefully when you hear a bird drumming in the woods. Try to pinpoint where the noise comes from, and then walk slowly and quietly in that direction. Grouse drum at intervals of several minutes, so be patient. If you walk up on the drumming log while the bird is silent, it may just sneak away. Move ahead a short distance and then wait until the grouse drums again. Usually the grouse will drum several times before you are able to get close enough to see it.

The grouse is a year-round denizen of the North Woods. Migration for grouse would be slow indeed. They are unable to fly far—a flushed grouse rarely travels much farther than one hundred yards—and, like chickens or ring-necked pheasants, spend most of their time walking. Researchers speculate that ruffed grouse are not found on Isle Royale because they are unable to fly the distance from the mainland.

Therefore the grouse has adapted to the rigorous conditions of a North Shore winter. Although they roost in conifers the rest of the year, during the winter grouse dive from trees to burrow beneath the snow. There the birds are hidden from predators. Snow, an excellent insulator, works together with fluffy feathers to keep grouse snug and cozy even on subzero northern nights. Observant skiers and snowshoers can see the tunnels of roosting grouse and may occasionally flush a bird from its winter hideaway.

Despite its familiarity—the ruffed grouse is found virtually everywhere on the North Shore—the bird remains mysterious. The late Gordon Gullion, famed Minnesota grouse researcher, made a breakthrough discovery when he outlined the relationship between grouse and aspen trees. The continental range of ruffed grouse and aspen closely overlap, and aspen buds, flowers, and leaves are important food sources. Gullion learned that timber harvesting could enhance populations of woodland species such as grouse and deer by providing lush young aspen growth adjacent to areas with mature trees.

However, not even Gullion could fully explain the grouse population cycle. About every ten years grouse populations reach peak abundance, only to dwindle to a low point a few years later. These ups and downs have been noted in other northern species, including snowshoe hares and lemming. Interestingly, the ruffed grouse population cycle is more pronounced in the northern portion of the bird's range.

The cycle is readily apparent to the ruffed grouse hunters who roam North Shore woodlands every autumn. When the birds are abundant, hunting is good. When the cycle is at a low point it can be a long walk between flushes.

Or a long drive. In recent years "roadhunters" have proliferated along the North Shore. Instead of walking trails and old logging roads to find their birds, they drive the forest roads and take potshots at grouse they see picking for gravel or feeding on roadside clover.

Of several possible reasons why roadhunting has grown in popularity, none are pleasant to contemplate. First is the public's preference for doing things the easy way. Second is the growing popularity of all-terrain vehicles, which many want but few need. Third is the tremendous amount of Forest Service road improvements in recent years, which have made it possible to take the family sedan nearly everywhere in the Superior National Forest but the BWCAW. Fourth is that grouse hunters, like cross-country skiers, mountain bikers, and sightseers, have finally "discovered" the North Shore.

Yet the majority of North Shore grouse see few if any hunters during the course of the season. Those hunters willing to venture off the beaten track usually have the forest to themselves. Walking hunters, especially those who use trained dogs, often have good shooting. Look for logged-over areas where the young aspen are no thicker than your wrist. In addition to grouse you may also flush woodcock.

Most epicures agree the ruffed grouse is the finest fowl to grace a dinner table. The white flesh has a delicate flavor that far surpasses grocery store chicken. One grouse per serving is about right.

Despite its delicious taste, most grouse lovers will tell you that the bird need not be eaten to be enjoyed. Distant drumming gives a welcome sign of spring. The sight of puffball grouse chicks will bring a smile to even the most mosquito-ridden early summer hiker. And nothing can kick-start a winter morning like a grouse thundering out from beneath your snowshoe. Without the ruffed grouse the North Shore would be a very different place.

Onion River

MILEPOST 86 It doesn't look like much from the highway. You can barely see the Onion—a river in name only. Yet follow the muddy path from the parking lot upstream a short distance and you'll reach a terraced waterfall. The path follows the canyon rim, so keep an eye on the kids.

The state property at Onion River is dedicated to lumberman Ray Berglund and is managed by the DNR's state parks division. Plans have been made to build a stairway up the bank from the parking lot and improve the trail to the waterfalls. Until then, this beautiful spot will belong only to those unafraid to get some dirt on their shoes.

The view from above

On Highway 61, a mile beyond the Onion you'll see a sign for the Superior Hiking Trail. Turn north from the highway on Forest Road 336 and follow it about two miles to the hiking trail parking lot. Lying on opposite sides of the Onion River are Leveaux and Oberg mountains. The summits of both can be reached via well-traveled hiking trails, considered by many to be two of the best hikes on the North Shore.

The Oberg trail is accessible to anyone in average physical condition, and benches provide places to rest. The trail switchbacks to the top of the mountain and circles the summit. Numerous overlooks provide five-star views of Lake Superior and the Sawtooth Mountains. You should allow about two hours for the hike.

The Leveaux trail is somewhat longer, but you can make a round trip in less than three hours. Although still accessible to most anyone, this trail is more strenuous. Plan to take a break on the climb to the summit. Your reward for reaching the top will be a spectacular North Shore panorama. Both trails are at their best during September, when the sugar maple ridges blaze with color.

The North Shore Mountains Ski Trail System

North Shore residents will tell you that cooperation is vital to the success of their small communities. Such cooperation brought the North Shore Mountains ski trail system to fruition. This labyrinth of groomed trails extends from Schroeder to Cascade State Park, and up to eight miles inland. A total of 196 kilometers of ski trails cross a mixture of federal, state, and private lands. Elevation varies as much as one thousand feet between lakeshore trails and trails crossing Sawtooth Mountain ridges.

Letters of the alphabet designate each trail in the system.

Signs mark intersections, and an excellent series of five maps shows land contours. Numerous trailheads lead to an endless choice of skiing possibilities. All trails are groomed at least once a week. Most are single-tracked, with double tracks near major trailheads. Ski-skating is possible on the long trail between Poplar River and Cascade State Park, as well as near Bally Creek and Oberg Mountain. There are plans to widen more trails for skaters.

Early and late in the winter the best skiing is on inland trails, where snow conditions are better. Near Lake Superior it may be Christmas before there's enough snow for skiing, and it rapidly disappears during March. Inland, diehards are able to ski from Thanksgiving (or earlier) into April.

The system is best described as lots of ups and downs. However, beginners shouldn't feel intimidated. Ask locally for direction to the easier trails, such as the Sugarbush and Oberg Mountain loops. Be sure the information you receive is up-to-date. Icy conditions can turn even a novice loop into an expert run.

Although the system is well used, don't expect to see many skiers when you get beyond the trailhead. For this reason you should ski smart. Tell someone where you are going and when you plan to return. Carry matches, an extra pair of socks, some candy bars, and your Minnesota ski pass. Remember that the sun sets quickly in the winter. Plan to be out of the woods well before dark. If you get lost, just start downhill. Eventually you'll end up at Lake Superior.

North Shore weather can be brisk, but don't let the cold deter you from skiing. Most of the trails wind through the woods and are sheltered from the wind. When the mercury dips below zero, plan shorter outings and stick to trails close to Lake Superior, where the temperature is significantly warmer than inland. The exercise associated with skiing often will keep you comfortably warm.

White-tailed deer are so common along the trails you could almost say they're a nuisance. The deer use the packed ski trails like sidewalks. So do wolves and coyotes, although few skiers are lucky enough to see these wild canines. However, enormous pileated woodpeckers are frequently sighted. In order to avoid disturbing wildlife and skiers, dogs are not allowed on the trails.

The rivers—skiing on the wild side

The most exciting North Shore skiing is done on the surfaces of frozen rivers. Traveling easily through secluded canyons and remote valleys, you can reach places rarely visited by anyone other than summer trout anglers. In many places you won't even see tracks from other skiers.

River skiing is challenging, even dangerous. Although the streams are shallow, you still chance hypothermia if you break through the ice and fall in. Bold skiers can jump small ledges and waterfalls. Those less sure of their abilities can take their skis off and climb around.

The most popular skiing stream is the Cascade. You can start from the bridge on the Pike Lake Road and ski down to Highway 61. Expect some challenges and be careful near open water.

Travel up the Poplar River for a more placid trip. Continue upstream from the footbridge that crosses the river about a half-mile above the ski hill. From there you can go upstream several miles and then head overland to the Caribou Trail. Carry a good map the first time you try it. Every river offers possibilities. For instance, the Onion upstream of Highway 61 is a fun ski.

You can also go inland and ski across lakes or follow forest roads. Late winter lake skiing is fast and fun. If you ski near clear-cut areas you may see moose. Look around carefully in places where you see lots of moose tracks and have good visibility. Keep a respectful distance from moose when you see them. They're ornery critters, and can make unprovoked charges. Deep snow doesn't deter them.

Lutsen Resort

MILEPOST
89

At the turn of the century C. A. Nelson, a commercial fisherman who lived at the mouth of the Poplar River, hosted a group of moose hunters from Duluth at his "Lutzen House." Moose were plentiful, and the sportsmen so enjoyed their stay at the Nelson homestead that they told their friends. A new North Shore industry was born. Lutsen is considered the North Shore's oldest resort. In addition to hunters and anglers, early guests included hayfever sufferers and tuberculosis patients. Guests and supplies arrived by boat, going by skiff from the ship to the large rock offshore from the resort. A long dock connected the rock to the shoreline. The resort prospered, becoming a year-round facility with the development of the ski hill in the 1950s. Architect Edwin Lundie designed the present Swedish-style main lodge, built in 1952.

Lutsen Mountains

Lutsen Mountains claims to offer the most mountainlike skiing in the Midwest. From the 1,688-foot summit of Moose Mountain there is a 1,000-foot vertical drop to the floor of the Poplar River valley. The longest ski run is more than a mile long. And skiers and sightseers taking the tramway can ride in a gondola to the summit of Moose, a mile from the chalet.

Lutsen Mountains offers a long ski season. The hill opens Thanksgiving weekend and usually has skiable snow until the first week of April. Artificial snowmaking complements Mother Nature's bounty. In addition to downhill skiing, winter wanderers can enjoy dogsled rides, sleigh rides, and cross-country skiing.

You can't ski in the summer, but you can still enjoy a fast run by piloting a sled down the serpentine course of Eagle Mountain's Alpine Slide. Or ride the gondola to the top of Moose Mountain, where you'll find a picnic area and an observation deck. The gondola is especially popular in the fall when the hills are ablaze with color. Summer and fall dogsled rides are also available.

Until recently, the only golf courses on the North Shore were nine-hole municipal facilities at Two Harbors, Silver Bay, and Grand Marais. The nearest eighteen-hole courses were in Duluth and Thunder Bay. Tourism promoters in the Lutsen-Tofte area thought a quality golf course would add to the attractiveness of their ski-country resorts during the summer months. They approached county officials and together planned a publicly funded championship golf course. Superior National at Lutsen opened in 1991.

Designed by golf course architect Don Herfort, Superior National follows the contours of the Poplar River valley just north of Highway 61. The river comes into play on several holes. Players have frequent vistas of Lake Superior, the Sawtooth Mountains, and river cascades. The course is a par seventy-two, and local promoters are not shy about calling it one of Minnesota's finest.

The playing season depends on weather, but usually extends from mid-May through mid-October. Try the course during the midweek; weekends you may need reservations.

Course managers plan to develop the area for other uses, including cart rides and hiking trails for nongolfers. Beginner-friendly ski trails crossing the course may be lighted for night skiing. Tobogganers have discovered a great sliding hill, and a skating rink is planned.

Superior National at Lutsen

It is difficult to envision the North Shore without white-tailed deer. They're everywhere, it seems. You can see them from the highway and you'll encounter them along hiking trails. In the winter their tracks obliterate groomed ski trails. Body shops do booming business repairing deer-damaged vehicles.

White-tailed Deer: North Shore Newcomers

Yet when pioneers first began venturing up the Shore during the 1850s, no whitetails were here. Instead, woodland caribou and moose populated the forest. However, settlement and logging brought changes to the land. Settlers hunted the plentiful caribou for food, and logging activities destroyed habitat. Slash that remained after cutting provided fuel for fires that raged across vast areas. New growth then surged on the burned land, creating ideal whitetail habitat.

The coming of white-tailed deer delivered the final blow to the caribou and moose. With the deer came brainworm, a parasite fatal to caribou and moose. That disease, combined with overshooting, brought a rapid decline to moose and caribou populations. By the 1920s both species had become scarce. The northeastern Minnesota moose season was curtailed in 1923. The following year marked one of the final caribou sightings, a lone animal seen along Lake Superior near Grand Portage Indian Reservation.

We know little about Minnesota's caribou. Apparently they made short migrations to wintering grounds, but no one ever mapped those areas, although it is known that caribou wintered along Hat Point near Grand Portage. Seagull Lake off the Gunflint Trail may have been another wintering area as caribou antlers have been found in that vicinity.

We also know little as well of the whitetail's early history on the Shore. By the 1930s large deer populations lived in the area from Lake Superior to the Canadian border. During the 1930s and 1940s the Shore gained renown as a deer hunting area.

As the second growth forest matured, deer numbers began to decline. By the early 1960s the forest had passed its prime as deer habitat. When severe winters in the late 1960s and early 1970s knocked the bottom out of the herd, the maturing habitat wasn't able to support a recovery.

Suddenly, it seemed, deer disappeared from the inland areas. They were replaced by moose, and a hunting season was reestablished for that species in 1971. Minnesota deer management and hunting seasons were restructured, and bucks-only hunting became law.

Hunters had difficulty accepting what had happened to the deer herd. They placed much of the blame on the timber wolf, which had been bountied until 1968. Forests mature so slowly that humans don't notice the change.

Obviously, however, whitetails didn't disappear from the North Shore. Now deer predominate in the area ten to fifteen miles inland from the lake. Moose inhabit the rest of the forest. Why?

In the winter, deer migrate to the south-facing hillside rising from Lake Superior. Snow depths are considerably lower there, and the lake moderates the winter climate. This climatic benevolence, combined with winter feeding by North Shore residents, allows deer to prosper. Moose are better adapted to survive the deep snows and cold temperatures found inland.

The places where deer congregate in the winter are called yards. Perhaps best known along the North Shore is the Jonvick deer yard near Cascade River. In 1948, during the whitetail's heyday, studies found 335 deer per square mile in Jonvick. Present counts are now over 100 deer per mile. The DNR improves habitat in the Jonvick yard to ensure that the deer have enough to eat.

North Shore deer face many perils, including life on Highway 61. The deer often cross the highway to reach feeding stations near homes or natural feeding areas. During the morning and evening hours they file back and forth across the highway like so many school children—without the benefit of a safety patrol. Although the lives of many deer are lost along the highway, they don't die in vain. Important scientific data has been collected from road-killed deer. Some carcasses are salvaged by local residents. Others feed the ever-hungry wolves, coyotes, foxes, ravens, chickadees, gray jays, red squirrels, and even bald eagles.

Early spring is an especially dangerous time for deer and

drivers. The snow melts first in the ditches and on exposed hillsides along the highway. Deer flock to these places to feed on the nutritious grasses, and business soars at the auto body shops.

Whitetails must also contend with predators. Both coyotes and timber wolves are common along the Shore, and they follow the deer to the yards. A study in the Lutsen area during the 1970s found the highest densities of timber wolves ever recorded. Unverified cougar sightings also occur in the area every year.

The whitetail's future along the North Shore is directly linked with forest management and winter weather. A current logging practice—clear-cutting—benefits forest wildlife such as deer and moose. Foresters now plan timber sales with the needs of wildlife in mind. Deer thrive if habitat is available, and the population can recover following severe winters. Whitetails have found a niche on the North Shore and it looks like they're here to stay.

What about caribou?

In the early 1980s, woodland caribou mysteriously reappeared along the North Shore. One or two small bands of caribou wintered in the Hovland area, where, for two years, they were seen by local residents. Then they disappeared.

Unverified caribou sightings have been reported over the years in the North Shore region. Animals may occasionally wander down from Ontario, where scattered small herds live. However, these few individuals will never add up to an established population. Ontario's caribou are found far north of the Minnesota border, and encroaching civilization threatens their habitat. Also, caribou that mingled with whitetails would likely contract the deadly brainworm.

Plans have been proposed to attempt restocking caribou into a remote area of the BWCAW. Biologists hope the caribou will swim to islands to give birth to their calves, because there they would be safe from predators such as wolves. The project, even though it has no guarantee, is the best hope we have of ever seeing caribou return to the state.

Lutsen

MILEPOST 90 In 1632 the Swedish king Gustavus II Adolphus was killed in battle at Lutzen, Germany. One of the generals who accompanied the king into battle and survived, Count Axel Gustafsson Lillie received property near Norrkoping, Sweden, on which to build an estate. Two centuries later, Carl Axel (Charlie) Nelson was born to one of the estate's peasant farming families. Faced with a grim future in Sweden, he came to Minnesota as a young man. He worked for a time in Minneapolis and Duluth, and then turned down an offer to work for the Merritts of iron mining fame in order to become a fisherman for the Booth Company. In 1885 he homesteaded at the mouth of the Poplar River. In 1890 he became the first postmaster of the community of Lutsen, which grew quickly, with homesteads both along the lake and inland.

Lutsen is now the center of a fast-growing tourist community. In fact, most of the recent tourism development along the North Shore has been in the Lutsen-Tofte area. Promoters boast of several fine restaurants and accommodations ranging from condos to bed-and-breakfasts. Vacation homes line the lakeshore, and shoreline land values along what locals call the Gold Coast are among the highest on the North Shore.

The Caribou Trail

MILEPOST 92 The Caribou Trail heads north from Highway 61 about a mile east of "downtown" Lutsen. The road is paved inland to Caribou Lake and then is gravel the rest of its twenty-mile length to the intersection with the Grade (Forest Road 153). Drive west two miles on the Grade and you'll reach Forest Road 326, which six miles North meets Brule Lake on the threshold of the BWCAW.

119

The Caribou is less traveled than the Sawbill or Gunflint trails, but several points of interest lie along the route. At the top of the ridge above Lake Superior you'll pass through a stand of old-growth sugar maple. West of the trail, a portion of the stand has been designated as a research site by the United States Forest Service. A walk through this forest—spectacular during the fall color season—takes you along the Superior Hiking Trail and on to Agnes Lake. The trail passes along the lake's north shore, where you'll find places to catch some sun while lying on lakeside rocks.

The Superior Hiking Trail will guide you to the top of White Sky Rock. White Sky, son of Jim Gesick, an Indian who lived near Lutsen, was the first state forest ranger hired in Cook County. The rock was named in White Sky's memory following his death from tuberculosis at the age of twenty-five.

Caribou Lake is popular with boaters and anglers. The lake is home to many cabins and also to Cathedral of the Pines, a large Lutheran summer camp. A number of other lakes, many with healthy walleye populations, are accessible from the trail. You can inquire locally about fishing guides.

Eagle Mountain

As mountains go, it's not much. But Minnesotans are proud of it. Eagle Mountain, at 2,301 feet above sea level, is Minnesota's highest point. On a clear day you can see Minnesota's lowest point from the summit: Lake Superior, with an elevation of 602 feet.

A round-trip hike to the top of Eagle Mountain takes half a day. The trailhead is off the Grade (Forest Road 153) about four miles east of the Caribou Trail intersection. A small lot provides parking on the north side of the road. From there you can follow the rocky three-and-a-half-mile trail to the top. Most of the trail is within the BWCAW, but you don't need a permit unless you plan to camp. Two designated campsites are at Whale Lake.

The trail is easy to follow, rocky in some places and wet in others, with planking across the boggy areas. Along the way you'll pass an old logging camp on Whale Lake, where you can see the remains of an old cabin. Beyond Whale Lake the trail climbs until you are on top of the Eagle Mountain bluffs. The last distance to the summit is marked with small piles of rocks. You'll know you've arrived when you find the metal monument plaque.

Is it worth it? Most hikers would say yes. Paddlers in the BWCAW rarely get a chance to look across an expanse of the canoe country. From the bluffs you can see several lakes and the distant Misquah Hills. If possible, pick a clear, sunny day for your hike so that you get the best view.

Berry Bounty

Blueberries rarely come easy. First you have to beat bears, birds, and other pickers to the patch. Then you have to spend a summer afternoon hunched over a bucket. It seems to take forever to pick enough berries to cover the bottom of the pail. Your back becomes stiff as the berries slowly accumulate. Some quit when they've picked enough for a fresh pie. Others keep at it until they've filled several containers with sweet berries. Still others just pluck and munch—often to the exasperation of their fellow pickers.

Blueberries grow widely in North Shore forests. Berry crops vary each year, but persistent pickers can usually find enough to fill a pail. The key is knowing where to look for them. Blueberries prefer sandy soils. Look for them near stands of jack pine or red pine. If the underbrush is sparse, you may find them growing beneath the pines. Otherwise look in nearby forest openings, such as old burns or cutovers. Often roadside areas will be picked over, while a short walk will lead you to berries in abundance.

If you are unsure about your berry-seeking abilities, stop in the Forest Service offices in Tofte or Grand Marais Foresters conduct regular burns in certain areas to improve berry habitat. The Forest Service folks can direct you to a patch. However, don't expect them to give away the locations of their favorite places. Blueberry pickers are just as secretive as brook trout anglers.

You can start finding ripe blueberries early in July on sunny hillsides, but the best picking is usually in the latter part of the month. Berries in deeply shaded areas or along the Lake Superior shoreline may not ripen until well into August. Berry patches are not created equal. The berries need sufficient moisture to reach pleasing plumpness. Late frosts can destroy the crop in exposed areas, and in some places wild critters eat the berries as quickly as they ripen.

Sweet wild raspberries ripen around the same time as blueberries. Because they are larger and grow on waist-high bushes, raspberries are easier to pick. They are often abundant in recent cutovers and other areas where a disturbance has created an opening in the forest.

Wild strawberries ripen in June and early July. The best place to look for these exquisitely flavored berries is along the roadside. Strawberries grow on vines within an inch or two of the earth. Picking enough for a strawberry shortcake is a good measure of your berry-picking stamina.

A local favorite is the juneberry, also called serviceberry. Contrary to its name, this berry ripens in July and August. Ripe juneberries are blue-black and look like very large blueberries. Birds find them so tasty they may clean off a bush before you have a chance to pick it. Juneberries grow on shrubs that reach fifteen or twenty feet in height. Look for them on the brushy edges of forest openings, such as around gravel pits.

In these same areas you may also find chokecherries and pincherries. Ripe chokecherries are deep purple and hang in grapelike clusters. Pincherries are red and grow in bunches. Both are used in jams, jellies, and wines.

Some folks live in perpetual fear of encountering a bear in the berry patch. Yes, it happens, but you are far more likely to be stung by a bee. Few people will let the outside chance of a bee sting keep them from enjoying the outdoors. Of course, bears are a bit larger than bees, but you still have little cause for alarm.

If you do happen upon a bear, most likely it will run off. Black bears are usually shy, although some, especially if they've had contact with people, may not leave. If you meet such a bear, keep your distance. Black bears—the only kind you'll find here—rarely attack humans. However, they may click their teeth or make a bluff charge. The purpose of these maneuvers is to frighten you, and they usually work.

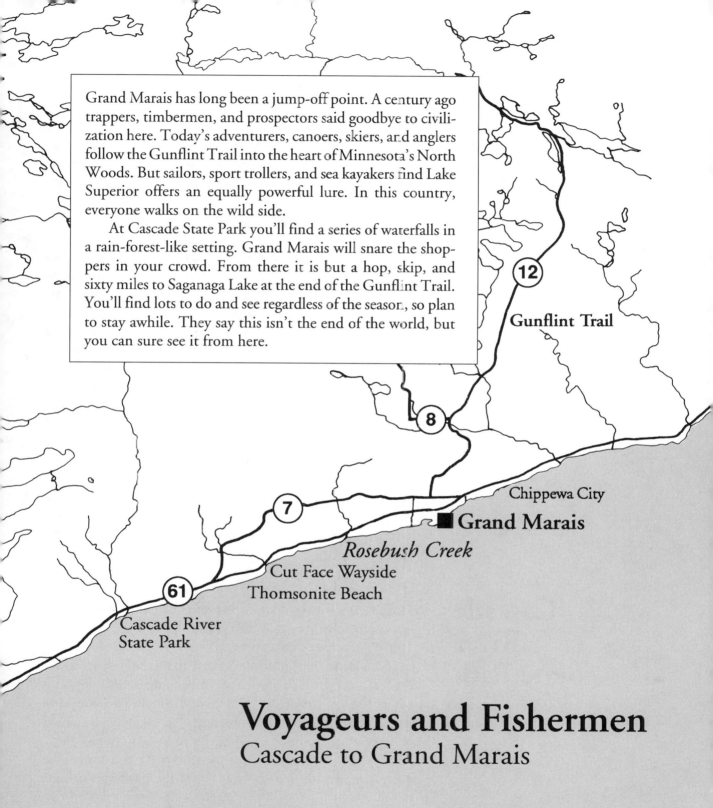

Grand Marais has long been a jump-off point. A century ago trappers, timbermen, and prospectors said goodbye to civilization here. Today's adventurers, canoers, skiers, and anglers follow the Gunflint Trail into the heart of Minnesota's North Woods. But sailors, sport trollers, and sea kayakers find Lake Superior offers an equally powerful lure. In this country, everyone walks on the wild side.

At Cascade State Park you'll find a series of waterfalls in a rain-forest-like setting. Grand Marais will snare the shoppers in your crowd. From there it is but a hop, skip, and sixty miles to Saganaga Lake at the end of the Gunflint Trail. You'll find lots to do and see regardless of the season, so plan to stay awhile. They say this isn't the end of the world, but you can sure see it from here.

12

Gunflint Trail

8

Chippewa City

■ **Grand Marais**

Rosebush Creek

7

Cut Face Wayside
Thomsonite Beach

61

Cascade River
State Park

Voyageurs and Fishermen
Cascade to Grand Marais

Cascade Lodge

MILEPOST 99 The Cascade Lodge is not part of Cascade River State Park, but a private enterprise that dates to the mid-1920s, before the park existed. An older log lodge was torn down after the current main lodge opened in 1939. Three log cabins still in use predate the lodge.

Like most North Shore tourist facilities, the lodge has metamorphosed from seasonal to year-round operation. Winterization along the North Shore began when the Lutsen ski hill opened in 1948. Winter traffic surged when cross-country skiing gained popularity in the 1970s. Some of the first cross-country ski trails on the Shore were at Cascade State Park. Winterization is expensive, and most resorts have done it over a number of years. At Cascade Lodge the restaurant first stayed open through the winter in 1970, and gradual winterization of the resort continued for the next twenty years.

The restaurant and lodge display several North American big game trophies. No, they weren't shot around here. Most came from Alaska and the Northwest Territories. The Alaskan bull moose in the restaurant is larger than Minnesota trophies, and the caribou in the lodge is one of the largest on record.

Cascade River State Park

MILEPOST 100 Walk two blocks upstream from Highway 61 and you will see that the Cascade River is well-named as the river pitches off a cliff into a swirling plungehole far below. Continue upstream on the well-trod hiking trail and you will reach a beautiful, rain-forest-like place where the river cascades over mossy ledges. Yes, you have seen this place before—on postcards, calendars, and framed photographs. No photographer can resist this river.

But few, if any, of the people who make this short hike every year realize that the trail from the parking lot leads over what was once the river's mouth, the site of an early commercial fishing village. Crews from the CCC moved the mouth of the river in the 1930s when they constructed the stone highway bridge across the river. The stream channel once flowed where the outhouse now stands beside the parking lot. Below the highway you can see roadbed riprap that uses rock from Tofte's Carlton Peak.

The CCC workers who built the bridge lived at Spruce Creek Camp, where the campground is now located; you can still see the foundations of several buildings there. Cascade River Camp stood several miles upstream, where the Pike Lake Road now crosses the river.

Cascade State Park, which is ten miles long and includes twenty-eight hundred acres, is a magnet for hikers and cross-country skiers. Winter or summer you'll find more trails than you could explore in a weekend of nonstop trudging. You can follow the river several miles (and a few hundred feet in elevation) upstream via the Superior Hiking Trail on the east bank or along a park trail on the west side. The Superior Hiking Trail also leads six hundred feet uphill to the summit of Lookout Mountain. Allow at least a couple of hours for this walk, and carry a water supply. The panoramic views of the lake, the Sawtooths, and the river valley reward the huffing and puffing. In the winter a groomed ski trail of moderate difficulty leads to the top.

The ski trails at Cascade are groomed once a week or as needed following snows. Many of the trail loops lead uphill into the backcountry, some connecting with the North Shore Mountains ski trail system. Expect some exciting downhill runs as you make your way back to Highway 61. Adventurous skiers can kick and glide all the way to the maple ridges and cedar thickets south of Deeryard Lake. Those seeking a lesser workout find an easier network of trails that stay in the lower elevations near the lake. Skiers can almost count on seeing deer, which winter in the park.

Snowmobilers can use a parking lot for the North Shore

Trail, marked with a sign on Highway 61 about three-quarters of a mile west of Cascade Lodge. A spur trail follows the powerline from the parking lot to the lodge. Another trail extends north and connects with the North Shore Trail and the Lutsen system.

The stretch of the Cascade River below the first falls is popular with anglers, especially during the fall, when chinook salmon stocked by the Minnesota DNR return to attempt spawning. How many fish successfully spawn is uncertain. The river has little spawning habitat, and the fishing pressure is relentless. Anglers line the riverbanks throughout the September and October spawning run. The hooksters are a congenial bunch, but the concentration of huge salmon in a stretch of river slightly longer than a football field leads to inevitable crowding. You can get more elbow room during the spring rainbow trout run. Above the falls the river offers mediocre fishing for brook and rainbow trout.

The mouth of the Cascade River is a good place for shore anglers to try their luck throughout the year. Lake trout are most frequently caught, with occasional rainbow trout, chinooks, and coho salmon. Anglers often congregate where the river flows into the lake, but fish can be caught all along the shoreline. The best times to fish are dawn, dusk, and on dark days.

Campers have several options at Cascade. The campground has thirty-nine semimodern sites, with showers, flush toilets, electric hookups, and a trailer sanitation station. Those who'd rather rough it have five backpacking campsites from which to choose. The group camp has two sites. If the weather outside is frightful, park visitors can use an all-year shelter complete with four picnic tables and a woodstove. Seven picnic sites are located on the lakeshore.

Butterwort Cliffs

Butterwort Cliffs Scientific and Natural Area (SNA) begins at the intersection of County Road 7 and Highway 61 and runs east about a mile along the shoreline. You need a permit, available at Cascade State Park headquarters, to enter the area. Park in the lot on the north side of the highway.

The basalt cliffs along the shoreline provide habitat for butterwort *(Pinguicula vulgaris)* and several other rare plants. Butterwort, a carnivorous plant, traps insects in its yellow, sticky leaves. It grows in fragile vegetative mats that form in rock crevasses. They are easily damaged by the footsteps of careless humans. A species of the tundra, butterwort is found in Minnesota only at scattered locations along the North Shore between Two Harbors and the Canadian border. The Minnesota DNR lists butterwort as a species of special concern.

Butterwort can exist along the North Shore because of Lake Superior's influence on the climate. Suitable growing conditions may be limited to just a few square feet at any one location, what botanists refer to as "microhabitats." In the case of butterwort, the total suitable habitat in Minnesota may amount to no more than a few acres scattered along one hundred miles of shoreline.

The same is true for some other arctic and alpine plants that have found a suitable niche along Lake Superior's rocky coast. Hudson Bay Eyebright, *Euphrasia hudsonia,* which grows in cracks in the shoreline bedrock, was once used as a cure for eye ailments. Alpine bistort, *Polygonum viviparum,* is found near Grand Portage; its total Minnesota habitat may be less than one acre. It grows in vegetative mats on exposed shoreline rocks, a brutal environment.

Small false asphodel, *Tofieldia pusilla,* is listed as endangered in Minnesota. Four populations have been discovered in Cook County, of which three number fewer than thirty plants. Small false asphodel growing on the North Shore and Isle Royale are separated from others of their kind by four hundred miles of forest—the nearest known populations are on the shores of James Bay in northern Ontario. They also prefer bedrock habitat.

One variety of moonwort, *Botrychium lunaria,* a tiny fern found in boreal forests, is so rare in Minnesota that it has been identified in only two locations along the North Shore. One population has about a dozen plants, the other only two or three. Even rarer, perhaps extinct, is the wild heliotrope *Phacella franklinii,* which botanists have been unable to locate in recent years. Formerly it had been found on wooded slopes along the North Shore and on east-facing cliffs in the BWCAW.

In 1989, a three-acre addition to Butterwort Cliffs SNA was dedicated to Tom Savage, a board member of the Minnesota chapter of the Nature Conservancy and an advisor to the DNR regarding SNAs, Savage had a home in Lutsen and was a prime mover in the effort to protect the plants at Butterwort Cliffs.

If North Shore geology interests you, be sure to see the rock formations where small lumps of colorful thomsonite are imbedded in the basalt. Look, but don't touch. Collecting thomsonite on this property is strictly forbidden.

The Butterwort Cliffs SNA also contains an active herring gull nesting colony. The size of the colony began declining during the late 1970s, and one suspected cause was human intrusion. Please, leave the gulls alone.

Copper in them hills?

Few hikers who travel the rugged backcountry of Cascade State Park venture from the beaten path. In fact, about the only time such bushwhacking is feasible is in late autumn and early spring, when the foliage and insects that foil summer explorers are nonexistant.

In late fall a few years ago a man reported finding what is the park's most intriguing mystery—an old copper mine. Somewhere along the west side of the river, the man said, he discovered a tunnel and a hand cart. Park officials have yet to verify his discovery.

Adventure, anyone?

Thomsonite Beach

MILEPOST 103 The two-mile stretch of rocky beach east of Cascade State Park isn't the only place in the world where thomsonite is found, but is the best known. Elsewhere in the world this zeolite mineral, which forms in gas pockets within volcanic rock, is white. Here impurities such as iron and copper have colored the stones, resulting in shades of red, green, yellow, and brown. The North Shore's unique thomsonite deposit has received little public attention or protection.

Scotland contains the only other known deposit of the gem, and the thomsonite vein there has been mined out. The stone owes its name to Scottish chemist Thomas Thomson, who identified it in 1820.

Only one in one hundred thousand thomsonite stones is of gem quality, fetching two thousand dollars or more. The others are too soft to work or have fractures in them. The best stones come from Lake Superior, where wave action slowly frees them from the one-billion-year-old basalt. The best concentration is along about one mile of shoreline and extends inland two hundred to five hundred yards, where the thomsonite-bearing basalt disappears into the hillside beneath another lava flow. Maurice Feigal, who devoted his life to working with the stone, identified 140 varieties, or families, of thomsonite, each with a pattern as unique as a fingerprint.

Feigal and his wife, Tania, own Thomsonite Beach Motel, a "front," so to speak, for their lapidary operation. They have spent decades transforming pieces of thomsonite into jewelry. Inside the motel a small jewelery shop offers items for sale, as well as an extensive display of thomsonite. In one stone you can see the face of Smokey Bear, in another a perfectly formed numeral 5. Still others have been carefully polished to reveal exquisite patterns. Thomsonite is so soft it can't be tumbled, and sometimes the pattern disappears as the stone is polished. They have an ephemeral quality, eventually being ground to dust by the tumbling action of the waves and gravel.

Although the early explorers and traders knew about thomsonite, the iron-mining Merritt brothers were the first to commercially mine the stone. They sold thomsonite to England from a mine on Terrace Point. Early settlers also collected the stones, and some North Shore families have thomsonite that has been in the family for generations.

Also found along this stretch of beach is a related gemstone—lintonite, or Minnesota jade. Lintonite, which comes in every shade of green, was named for Dr. Linton, the woman who discovered it.

Cutface Wayside

MILEPOST 104 Just beyond Thomsonite Beach the highway crosses Terrace Point giving you a terrific view of Good Harbor Bay and distant Grand Marais. As the highway rounds the bay you'll see a small lakeshore wayside at the mouth of Cutface Creek—a great place to have a picnic and look for thomsonite along the beach (in fact, this is just about the only public area where you can collect thomsonite specimens).

Locals call this area the rock cut. Cutface Creek has worn away the softer material between two lava flows. The pines and spruce you see along the highway and in the wayside were planted following a fierce fire years ago. Farther up the slope, little but scrub grows. Time has yet to heal the scars of early settlement.

Fall River

MILEPOST 107 The only parking available at Fall River is along the shoulder, so be careful. Why stop? Because just below the highway there's a grottolike waterfall and a secluded beach.

Footpaths lead along both banks, but the one on the east side is the most traveled. When the water is low you can rock-hop across the creek to reach the gravel beach. When the water is high, walk down the west bank. Use caution near the waterfall, because the paths might be slippery. The shoreline adjacent to the stream mouth is public.

Locals know this stream as Rosebush Creek, because wild roses bloom along the banks in June. Rosehips, a fruit that ripens in the fall, are eaten by ruffed grouse, chipmunks, and other forest animals. Humans can eat them, too, but they aren't very tasty. However, they're good in jellies, and fermented, they make an exquisite sherry.

During the 1870s, two men mined several hundred pounds of native copper a mile and a half upstream. On occasion rockhounds have found native copper in this area. You might also find thomsonite along the beach.

Grand Marais

MILEPOST 109 Grand Marais is a slice of civilization wedged between Lake Superior and the Superior National Forest. Here the North Woods meets the modern world. Don't believe it? Just listen to the conversations you overhear while eating breakfast in a Grand Marais restaurant. At one table two woodsmen discuss beaver trapping, and at another artists talk about batik. Precisely this mixture of rough and refined defines Grand Marais and explains the community's diverse appeal.

Some say *grand marais* is French for "large marsh," but others, including Cook County historian Bill Raff, assert that the word *marais* actually meant "harbor" or "place of refuge." A gravel tombolo extends out to Artist's Point, which provides a natural breakwater for the town's harbor and also shelters the East Bay. Still, "marsh" is not far from the truth: downtown lies but three feet above lake level and occasionally floods during storms.

In 1823, John Jacob Astor's company established a fur-trading post and fishing camp at Grand Marais, but abandoned the endeavor by 1840. In 1854 white settlers came to

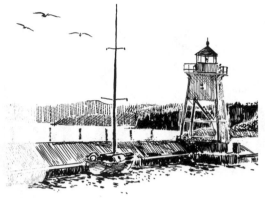

Grand Marais again following the signing of treaties with the Ojibwa. In 1856 a post office was established with Richard Godfrey as postmaster. Like others who ventured into the newly opened "Indian lands," Godfrey, a fisherman and prospector, expected to strike it rich. Copper had been discovered on the Upper Peninsula, and the new arrivals hoped to find it on the North Shore as well.

The Panic of 1857 dashed the hopes of most prospectors and settlers along the North Shore, and the post office, which had been renamed Hiawatha, officially closed on September 30, 1858. In 1870 and 1871, three men, Hazael (Henry) Mayhew, Sam Howenstine, and Ted Wakelin, became property owners. They are known as the founding fathers of Grand Marais. The first settlement, a cluster of cabins and wigwams, rose where the campground is today.

Henry Mayhew and his brother, Thomas, loom large in Grand Marais's early history. Thomas, a doctor and, some say, a Union spy during the Civil War, had a medical practice in Grand Marais and helped his brother operate a trading post. Patients and customers were trappers, prospectors, and fishermen. Although prospectors discovered both silver and gold across the border in Ontario, neither metal was mined here. However, stories go around about one old-timer who used to vanish into the backcountry once a year and return with enough gold nuggets to live on. No one has ever discovered where he found the gold.

Nearly all North Shore transportation was via steamers and sailing vessels, so Grand Marais's harbor was vital to the town. The east pier was constructed in 1883 and 1884, and the west pier was completed in 1904. The first lighthouse was built in 1886, and Joseph Mayhew, the doctor's son, became the first keeper. The Cook County Historical Society Museum is located in the lightkeeper's residence, constructed in 1896.

Gravel removal operations enlarged the harbor. In the days before bulldozers and backhoes, beaches provided an accessible source of gravel. Much of the gravel mined in the Grand Marais harbor was hauled by scow to Duluth, where it became a base for city streets.

By the turn of the century Grand Marais had been established as a summer tourist destination. Some came to hunt or fish, others to walk the beaches and woodlands. Graffitti from these early tourists can be seen chiseled in the shoreline rocks on the way to the lighthouse. Some of the inscriptions are nearly one hundred years old.

Culture in the woods

Grand Marais's natural beauty has long inspired artists. One of the first, Anna Johnson, wife of local entrepreneur Charles Johnson, came to the area in 1907. She painted North Shore scenes in watercolors and oils, and produced works in ceramics, china, and other media. She opened the first gift shop on the North Shore, where she sold some of her creations.

In 1947, Minneapolis artist Birney Quick founded the Grand Marais Art Colony. Over the years the colony has grown and gained recognition throughout the Midwest. In addition to a busy schedule of summer and fall workshops, the Art Colony also provides arts instruction for students in the Cook County school system. The work of artists associated with the colony can be seen throughout the community. Most prominent is the statue of two bear cubs in a tree, located on the harbor near the entrance to downtown. Raymond Gormley and his students created the sculpture in 1953. Innumerable paintings by colony artists grace the walls of local homes and businesses.

The new Johnson Heritage Post, a log structure built on the former site of Charles Johnson's trading post, celebrates Cook County's artists. On display are works by Anna Johnson and Birney Quick; former *Cook County News-Herald* editor, Ade Toftey, and photographer M. J. Humphrey, as well as internationally acclaimed native son George Morrison. The museum also features traveling exhibits.

Another cultural institution, the Grand Marais Playhouse, presents a series of performances during the summer. Most of the talent is local, but don't let that fact deter you from seeing a play. The productions are top-notch. Occasionally the playhouse schedules other stage and musical events. Check locally for a current schedule.

Downtown

In the summer, the most challenging part of a downtown Grand Marais excursion is finding a place to park. Try the side streets or the city parking lot across Broadway from the tourist information center. The center has information for all of Cook County. They can tell you about local events or help find a room when accommodations are tight.

Grand Marais offers something for every shopper. You can find souvenirs, T-shirts, artwork, sporting goods, clothing, books, and antiques. All shops are within easy walking distance, and restaurants with varied menus are interspersed among the stores.

Although you can easily occupy an afternoon shopping and snacking in Grand Marais, don't pass up a visit to the Cook County Museum, which has relics from Grand Marais's not-so-distant pioneer past. Displays of commercial fishing, early logging, and homesteading, show you what life was like when Grand Marais was accessible only by boat.

Stretch your legs

The wild side of Grand Marais is but a five-minute walk from downtown. The best-known nature trail is Artist's Point, a rocky outcrop east of the harbor which extends into the lake east of the harbor. Park near the Coast Guard Station on the point and walk from there. Paths to the east lead out onto Artist's Point. To the west you can walk along the breakwall to the harbor entrance.

The point is most pleasant on calm, sunny days and most beautiful on stormy ones. Deepwater rollers rise and crash on the rocks, creating excellent photo opportunities. Early birds can catch sunrise over the lake, and sunset over the Sawtooths, especially during winter, is spectacular. If you venture out on the point when the surf is up, be careful. Often waves go right over the breakwall and in the winter, icy rocks make walking treacherous. No matter the weather or the season, keep a close eye on the kids. Lake Superior is as dangerous as it is beautiful.

The less known, but scenic, Honeymoon Bluff trail, begins in the city recreation area on the west side of the harbor. To find the trailhead, go all the way through the park. The path begins unceremoniously behind the campground dumpsters then follows the lakeshore, climbing a rocky hill to offer a terrific view of the village and the lake. The complete loop is less than a mile and brings you back to where you started.

On the water

The residents of Grand Marais take great pride in their beautiful harbor. In the past, loggers rafted logs into giant booms, which were towed to mills across the lake. Generations of commercial fishermen used the port as a base for offshore lake trout and herring netting operations. Steamers hauling new immigrants and needed supplies stopped here.

Today the harbor's primary use is recreational. Get up early, especially in the spring and fall, and you may see a commercial fishing boat returning with a catch. However, you are more likely to see sport trollers and sailors heading out from the city-owned marina and public launch area. The Coast Guard maintains a seasonal station here to keep a watchful eye on boaters.

Grand Marais has two launch areas: a concrete ramp with a short protective wall on the west side of the harbor and a newer DNR access on the east side. Both are free and accommodate trailerable craft. The marina sells gas and other supplies. One drawback—the facility is often full, so berths and tie-up space are limited. Mooring is difficult because the harbor isn't fully protected, and sunken logs left over from the lumbering days have an appetite for anchors.

Grand Marais lies within cruising distance—about forty miles—from Isle Royale. Another popular destination is Bayfield, Wisconsin, seventy miles across the lake. You don't need your own boat to enjoy the water because you can rent sailboats and sea kayaks in Grand Marais. Excursions and seaplane rides are also available.

During July and August sport anglers congregate at Grand Marais to fish for coho salmon, which pass by during their annual summer migration. These feisty salmon, as well as chinooks and lake trout, can be caught near the surface during these months. In the spring and early summer, and again in the fall, lake trout make up the bulk of the offshore catch. If you don't have the necessary boat or equipment for fishing Lake Superior, inquire locally about charter services.

Winter fun

They used to say that Grand Marais rolled up the sidewalks after Labor Day and hibernated until the spring fishing opener. No more. Winter recreation in Grand Marais and Cook County now attracts intrepid vacationers from across the nation and winter events add to the fun.

Recently snowmobiling has become tremendously popular in Grand Marais. The town is well suited to sledders because spur trails allow you to go directly from your motel into the woods. In addition to an extensive groomed trail system through the Gunflint backcountry, Grand Marais is also linked to the North Shore State Trail. A parking lot for the trail system is near the county garage off County Road 7.

Dog Days

Grand Marais hosts an annual Dog Days winter carnival in January during the John Beargrease Sled Dog Race. Two middle-distance races, the Beargrease 90 and 130, begin downtown on Broadway. The afternoon start of these races, which draw dozens of teams, allows spectators an opportunity to get up close and personal with mushers and their dogs. Local merchants plan sales and other activities for the race day.

Gunflint Hills Golf Course

Hilly and wooded, the Gunflint Hills Golf Course offers a challenging nine holes. The par thirty-three course, located five miles north of Grand Marais on the Gunflint Trail, is open May through October. Early-morning golfers may see a moose amble across the fairways. In the fall, migrating geese occasionally land on the course to rest and feed.

Camp, swim, and shower

The popular Grand Marais Recreation Area has three hundred campsites available from May through October: 147 sites with full hookups, 104 sites with electric and water, and 36 primitive sites. The campground is on the west side of the harbor, a stone's throw from Lake Superior.

The recreation area includes an Olympic-sized indoor swimming pool, which is open to the public year-round. Swimmers can also enjoy a sauna and whirlpool. However, paddle-weary and mosquito-crazed voyageurs who are coming out of the BWCAW will find another amenity even more refreshing—hot showers. The recreation area has four bathhouses, with showers available for a small fee.

Picnic in the recreation hall on rainy days or listen to nature talks on summer evenings. Kids who tire of skipping stones in the harbor will find their way to the playground.

Fishermen's Picnic

Fishermen's Picnic, held in Grand Marais on the first weekend in August, is the North Shore's largest shindig. Begun during the 1920s as a get-together for commercial fishermen and their families, the picnic has become a quintessential small-town celebration, complete with a queen, a parade, and

Krazy Days. The hard-working Grand Marais Lion's Club sponsors today's picnics.

The picnic kicks off with a dinner Wednesday night, but the real fun starts on Thursday when merchants hold sidewalk sales. A stage platform is set up in Bear Tree Park, and entertainment continues throughout the four-day event. Street dances are held on Friday and Saturday nights, and on Friday evening the high school hosts the Miss North Shore contest.

Events of all sorts take place Saturday and Sunday: bed races, stone-skipping contests, and Saturday-night fireworks. A crowd favorite is the fish toss—similar to an egg toss, but the egg is replaced by a slimy dead herring. You'll be surprised how far a fish can fly. Sunday features a parade, and the picnic culminates with a grand prize drawing for a new car that afternoon.

Potential picnic-goers should plan ahead and book accommodations in advance. It's a cinch that rooms will be hard to find the week of the event.

Not tropical, but . . .

Want to know Grand Marais's best kept secret? It's warm during the winter.

Lake Superior's water temperature hovers just above freezing during the winter and moderates the North Shore climate. The mercury may bottom out thermometers inland, but temperatures near the lake will be twenty degrees warmer. That's why Grand Marais is often the warmest place on a Minnesota weather map in January.

Of course, what goes around comes around. During the summer the lake's cold water has the opposite effect. The state may be suffering through a heat wave, but it will still be chilly enough to require a jacket near the lake. Remember, they don't call it the air-conditioned North Shore without reason. Pack warm clothes for your visit, even during July and August.

Herring, Anyone?

You don't have to be Scandinavian to enjoy fresh herring, a North Shore delicacy. Virtually every restaurant in Grand Marais has herring on the menu. Quite often you'll find herring fillets at the meat counter in the local grocery stores, too.

You'll find herring prepared in several ways. Fried fillets are often served with potatoes and vegetables as a dinner entree. Or the fillets are slid into a bun, creating a herring sandwich. Smoked herring and cold beer make a combination that's hard to beat.

However, no herring connoisseur will pass up fishcakes, a traditional Scandinavian dish. Ground herring is mixed with eggs and spices, then shaped into patties and cooked. The taste is exquisite. The only problem is that fishcakes are often hard to find on restaurant menus. Most establishments feature fishcakes as an occasional daily special rather than a regular entree. But if you enjoy eating fish, a fishcake dinner is worth the search.

The Pincushion Trail System

The trailhead for the popular Pincushion trail system is two miles north of Grand Marais on County Road 53 off the Gunflint Trail. The parking area doubles as a scenic overlook, offering an excellent view of Grand Marais and the lake. However, the best view is from the summit of Pincushion Mountain, which is a five-mile round trip from the trailhead.

During the winter, Pincushion is a popular ski area. Although all levels of skiers can find suitable trails, most of the system was designed for intermediate and expert skiers. Twenty-five kilometers of groomed trails are marked at every intersection. Pincushion is usually skiable by early December and holds its snow through the end of March, receiving an average of ninety-two inches of snow annually. Twelve kilometers of trail are groomed for ski skating. The

Sawtooth Challenge, a cross-country ski race held each January, attracts over two hundred skiers each year.

The loop leading to Pincushion Mountain is the most interesting. Before reaching the mountain the trail follows the rim of Devil's Track canyon. In order to reach the top of Pincushion Mountain you must take off your skis and walk about a quarter mile to a rocky knob. From there you have a panoramic view of the canyon and the lake. On a clear day you can see Isle Royale, forty miles distant.

Locals say Pincushion Mountain was named about sixty years ago following a disastrous fire. The burnt remains of trees projected from the hill at all angles, making it resemble a pincushion. The forest has grown back during the last six decades. Now the trail winds through stands of birch and aspen, which shelter skiers from winter winds.

During the summer the trail is mowed for hikers and mountain bikers. Wet areas, once the nemesis of summer trail users, have been drained. Hikers can gain access from the Pincushion system to the Superior Hiking Trail. A round-trip hike to the top of Pincushion Mountain will take two or three hours. Mountain biking is not encouraged on the Superior Hiking Trail, but bikes are allowed on the Pincushion system. Novice bikers may find Pincushion's rolling topography more than they care to conquer. You can rent mountain bikes in Grand Marais.

Sea Kayaking

Lake Superior breathes. Even when the winds are still the waters softly heave, an incomprehensible primal force. We may not understand but we can see, hear, and feel Superior's power, and beneath a sea kayak, the lake comes alive.

To a novice, setting out on the mighty lake in such a seemingly frail craft may seem foolhardy. After all, didn't some guy sing about the lake never giving up its dead? Isn't the weather unpredictable, turning from serene to treacherous in moments? Superior is no wading pond, but Indians traversed its waters for centuries in birch-bark canoes. Regardless of whether you pilot an ore carrier or a kayak, boating on the big lake demands that you understand your capabilities and your craft's. Don't get cocky and you should stay out of trouble.

A sea kayak is not as frail as it first appears. In fact, the craft was originated by seagoing Arctic peoples for work and travel on northern seas. They are well suited to waters such as Superior. However, it takes awhile to become acquainted with a kayak. When you first ease into the water a kayak seems tippy, as if the slightest wave will cause it to overturn. After you've paddled over a couple of swells you realize the craft is quite stable. A new world opens before you.

To paddle a kayak on Superior is to become one with the lake. You ride low to the water, like a swimming gull, and you pitch and bob with the rolling swells. From the bottom of a swell you may not see a companion paddling just a few yards away. Then you rise to the crest of a wave and look far across the water. With a few paddle strokes you glide quickly forward.

The best way to make a close inspection of the shoreline is from a sea kayak. You can paddle along just beyond the breakers, unconcerned about reefs or rocks that could tear the prop off a powerboat. You will find gull rookeries (if the birds let you come near), weatherworn cedars, and shoreline homes. Look down and you can watch the changing patterns of lake-bottom rocks.

Sea kayaking is growing in popularity along the North Shore, even though some experienced kayakers feel that the Minnesota coast is less than ideal. Except for the Grand Portage area, few islands or sheltered bays are found. Touring is difficult because long stretches of beach are privately owned. Camping is essentially limited to state parks or other public areas. However, day-trippers can have lots of fun, and with prior planning the more adventurous will have dynamite overnight trips.

Newcomers to kayaking can get introductory instruction from some North Shore outfitters. This is the best way to learn the basics: how to enter a kayak, how to attach a spray skirt, and how to paddle. If you practice on a warm inland lake or are unafraid of a cold Superior ducking, you can learn the Eskimo roll. This maneuver allows you to easily upright an overturned kayak.

Classes also emphasize kayaking safety. Lake Superior is no place to make mistakes, because cold water is a quick killer. In the summer wearing a life vest may be sufficient, but spring and fall kayakers prefer the protection of a dry suit or wet suit. Pay close attention to the wind, and stay close to shore, because a strong offshore breeze could prevent your return. Winds can come up suddenly on the lake, but a smart boater can usually make it to shelter. It all gets down to staying within your capabilities.

Sea kayak rentals are available at several locations along the North Shore. However, growing numbers of people are buying their own. Many North Shore homeowners have found kayaking to be an excellent way to enjoy a quiet evening. Others like to test their skills in the surf. A good paddler can handle surprisingly rough water in a sea kayak.

Although you can go virtually anywhere with a kayak, some locations beat others. Launch at the mouth of the Baptism River in Tettegouche State Park and explore Shovel Point and the rock formations near Palisade Head. Farther north, paddle to the mouth of the Manitou River, which is privately owned, and see the waterfall that plunges directly into the lake. Explore the scenic cliffs east of Tofte. Play in the Grand Marais harbor or paddle around Artist's Point. Near the Canadian border, visit the Susie Islands, Wauswaugoning Bay, and Pigeon Point, with its Hole in the Wall cove.

If you want to make an overnight trip, consider the Gooseberry and Split Rock areas, which have substantial public beaches. In many areas east of Grand Marais the beaches are highway right-of-ways. If you camp there the drone of passing trucks may lull you to sleep.

If roughing it isn't your style, you could arrange to paddle from lodge to lodge. No resorts currently offer this package, but most will accommodate your needs if you plan in advance. Experienced paddlers make the several-hour journey to Isle Royale, but this passage isn't recommended for beginners.

Neither is long-distance touring. A handful of enthusiasts circumnavigate the lake each summer, and trips from point A to a distant point B are possible. Again, the Minnesota coast isn't the first choice of most paddlers. Much preferred is the wild Ontario shoreline, with its innumerable points, bays, and islands.

The Gunflint Trail

MILEPOST 109 You can measure the longevity of a North Shore oldtimer by how rugged the Gunflint Trail was as far back as he or she can remember. The entire sixty-mile length to the Seagull River is paved, but plenty of folks can remember when it was gravel—little more than a trail. Now you can easily drive to the end of the trail and back in a morning. However, you'll want to set aside at least a day to look this country over.

The Gunflint traverses the most spectacular landscape in Minnesota. Beginning in Grand Marais, it climbs to the top of Maple Hill, where Cook County pioneers eked out an existence by farming and logging. Civilization ends abruptly at the Hedstrom lumber mill, and the Gunflint plunges into the Superior National Forest. It winds over and around pine-clad granite ridges, crossing rivers and bogs. When the trail nears the halfway point at Poplar Lake it enters a corridor bounded on both sides by the Boundary Waters Canoe Area Wilderness (BWCAW).

The Gunflint country has stunningly beautiful lakes. Most are long and narrow, with high ridges rising up on either side. On some lakes, such as Clearwater and Hungry Jack, sheer palisades rise three hundred feet. Centuries of frost action have left huge talus piles beneath the cliffs. The waters, clear like those of Lake Superior, are inhabited by coldwater species such as lake trout, whitefish, northern pike, and suckers. Originally those were about the only fish in these border lakes, but people later stocked walleyes and smallmouth bass, which now successfully spawn in many lakes. Other species, especially brook trout, rainbow trout, and splake, cannot reproduce in lakes and must be stocked.

The Gunflint Trail has long appealed to anglers, who were among the first tourists to discover the area. Hundreds of lakes are accessible from the trail, albeit with varying degrees of difficulty. On some lakes, such as Devil Track, you can launch any trailerable craft. Others, such as Saganaga, have motor horsepower limits, and you are required to get a free permit from the Forest Service. Still others, such as Birch, require you to carry your small boat or canoe down a short (but often steep) path from the parking area. And lakes like Tuscarora can be reached only by paddling and portaging into the BWCAW.

The resort and outfitting businesses used to cater primarily to anglers. Some still do, but others now attract a broad and year-round clientele. The Gunflint is now on the map as an exotic destination, appealing to the jet-setting eco-tourist as well as the weekend angler from Duluth. The Gunflint offers so much more than just fishing.

For instance, the Gunflint is renowned for cross-country skiing. You can count on deep, fluffy snow every winter. Heavy snowfalls in October aren't unusual, but the ski season gets rolling around Thanksgiving. February is the most popular month.

Skiers have three interconnected groomed trail systems from which to choose, as well as Pincushion near Grand Marais. Resorters provide such skiing options as lodge-to-lodge trips, evening skiing by lantern light, and backcountry

skiing to Mongolian yurts (warm, walled tents). You can also make day or overnight trips into the BWCAW.

Another popular winter sport is snowmobiling. A network of well-groomed trails allows you to ride from Grand Marais to the Canadian border at Saganaga Lake. In the talking stage is a trail from Sag (as the big lake is known) to Thunder Bay. Many snowmobilers combine trail riding with winter fishing.

Before the snowmobiling era, dog teams provided winter travel in the Gunflint country. The sound of barking sled dogs again rings through the hills, with local mushers offering both short rides and extended trips into the winter wilderness. Mushing through the BWCAW is a hands-on experience, because vacationers are allowed to handle the teams. As they cross the frozen lakes dogsledders occasionally see wolves on the ice.

The Gunflint Trail is plowed throughout the winter, but drive with care. Not only are there icy patches, but often you'll round a corner to find a moose in the road. The moose, attracted by the salt applied to the roadway, get down on their knees to lick the pavement. No thrill quite matches swerving to avoid a kneeling moose.

Unlike on Highway 61, deer are uncommon along the Gunflint Trail. The only large herd is at Gunflint Lake, where local residents feed them through the winter.

Spring is a quiet season along the Gunflint, a time when resorters vacation and prepare for the upcoming summer. The state fishing opener in mid-May kicks off the summer tourist season. However, because of motor restrictions and the fishing closures in walleye spawning areas, the trail attracts fewer anglers than it once did. Many anglers pursue native lake trout, which are found in shallow water during the spring, or stream trout, which have been stocked in dozens of lakes. Every spring a handful of lucky anglers catch brook trout in the three- and four-pound range.

Whether or not you like to fish, spring is an excellent

time to explore the Boundary Waters Canoe Area Wilderness. Spring brings out fewer people and fewer biting insects than do the summer months. (Generally, blackflies become troublesome during the latter part of May, and mosquito swarms soon follow.) The ice occasionally doesn't leave the lakes until well into May, and spring snowfalls are not unusual so leave the shorts and suntan lotion at home. Springtime paddlers wear woolens and come prepared for inclement weather.

Summer, though short, is certainly more benign, with warm days and cool nights. During June and July, evening seems to last forever. Lush scents permeate the air and loons call across still lakes. In weedy bays you may happen upon feeding moose standing in the water. Many choose to take canoe trips at this time of year. The fishing isn't bad either, especially for smallmouth bass, walleyes, and northern pike.

By the end of August you can feel the nip of fall in the air. The leaves begin changing by early September and hit a color peak during the latter part of the month. Autumn is a prime time to explore the Gunflint's many miles of hiking trails. You can take hikes ranging in length from a couple of hours to a couple of days. A favorite short walk, the Honeymoon Bluff Trail, starts on County Road 66 near the Flour Lake Campground. The trail is steep, but not particularly strenuous. The view from the bluff, looking across Hungry Jack Lake, will take your breath away. The lake was named one winter during the 1870s when a woodsman named Andrew Jackson "Jack" Scott spent a couple of weeks there waiting for other members of his government survey crew to return with supplies. His food supplies ran low, and he was forced to catch snowshoe hares for his meals. When his companions returned, they asked, "Are you hungry, Jack?" to which they received a lusty reply.

Another popular trail is the mile and a half walk to Magnetic Rock. It crosses Larch Creek and an old forest burn on the way to the big stone. Why do they call it

Magnetic Rock? Carry a compass and see for yourself. If flora and fauna interest you, explore the three nature trails along the Gunflint: a wildflower trail near the Devil Track River crossing and nature trails at the Flour Lake Campground and at Seagull Landing.

Longer trails lead into the BWCAW. You don't need a permit for day hikes, but you do if you plan to stay overnight. Hiking isn't very popular among BWCAW users, so you will probably find privacy. Best known is the Border Route Trail, which follows high granite ridges as it winds between the border lakes. You can gain access to the Border Route from several locations along the Gunflint. For an interesting—and rugged—day hike start on the Caribou Rock/Split Pines Trail off the Hungry Jack Road. As you hike the four miles to the Stairway Portage between Duncan and Rose lakes you'll see West Bearskin and Moss lakes. Walk east from the Stairway Portage on the Border Route Trail, then climb to the top of a palisade above Rose Lake. From there you can look across Rose into Canada.

Hikers confident in their backwoods abilities can tackle the Kekekabic Trail, which crosses the BWCAW between the Gunflint Trail and Ely. Volunteer groups maintain the Kekekabic, and keeping up with the deadfalls is a constant battle. In places the trail becomes difficult to follow. However, dayhikers can easily walk in a couple of miles to the site of the Old Paulson Mine. More information about the Kekekabic and all Gunflint hiking trails is available at the United States Forest Service Gunflint District Ranger Station in Grand Marais.

Of course, seeing the beauty of a North Country autumn from the comfort of a vehicle satisfies some. The Gunflint doesn't have the extensive maple stands found in other locations along the North Shore, but leaf lookers can investigate a couple of routes. As the Gunflint crests the hill above Grand Marais it passes through a maple forest. Continue north for a couple miles on the Trail and then turn east

on County Road 60 near Hedstrom's mill. Maples border this gravel road for several miles. You can turn south on County 14 to meet Highway 61 near Kimball Creek. Or you can continue on 14 and turn north on the Trout Lake Road, which winds through some beautiful country before intersecting with the Gunflint Trail.

Exploring the Gunflint backroads becomes less of an adventure every year. The Forest Service has spent millions reconstructing forest roads in order to make them passable by any vehicle from a sports car to semi trucks. The result has been needless convenience and the taming of Minnesota's North Woods.

One example is Forest Road 313, a wide, gravel highway that connects the Gunflint with Arrowhead Trail north of Hovland. Even concrete-bound city slickers would have trouble getting lost on this route. A loop trip takes two or three hours, and you're likely to see moose and other wildlife along the way—especially early in the morning or in the evening. Follow the Gunflint north to Greenwood Lake Road, just beyond the bridge over the South Brule River. Drive east on the Greenwood Lake Road to the Assinika Creek crossing and then turn north on 313. Follow 313 through to the Arrowhead Trail and then turn south to return to Highway 61. Recent logging activity has left large clear-cut areas along this route. These openings provide excellent places to look for moose and black bears. You may also see ruffed grouse, pine marten, red fox, or other animals along the way. There are never guarantees in wildlife watching, but this route is consistent.

If forest land management interests you, stop in the Gunflint District Ranger Station for a copy of the guide to the South Brule Road, which goes west from the Gunflint. The Forest Service, in cooperation with Hedstrom Lumber Company, has produced a brochure that explains the history, vegetation, wildlife habitat, and forest management practices that are visible from the roadside. A surprising diversity in the landscape becomes apparent when you read the brochure.

The Gunflint pines

Ten miles north of Grand Marais the Gunflint Trail passes through a stand of two-hundred-year-old white pine. Once common in Minnesota, white pine forests remain in less than one percent of their original acreage. The tree was prized for its lumber—so prized it was logged nearly to extinction.

The parklike appearance of the Gunflint pines is not natural. In 1990 the Forest Service removed the vegetation beneath the pines. Much of this growth was balsam that had succumbed to the spruce budworm. The agency will plant white pine seedlings beneath the giants.

Roads and railroads

The first white explorers to penetrate the Gunflint country were interested less in the region's natural beauty than its natural riches. Trappers and prospectors crisscrossed the area in the latter half of the nineteenth century. Fur had been important to the area economy for centuries, and it took little imagination to envision the rocky hills as full of yet-to-be-discovered mineral wealth. Discoveries of silver and gold in nearby Ontario added further incentive.

In the 1870s pioneer prospector Henry Mayhew established a fur-trading post at Rove Lake, on the Canadian border north of Grand Marais. He used Indian crews to cut a rough trail between the post and his facility at Grand Marais. A member of the county board of commissioners, he convinced other local officials that the county should fund improvements to his trail. These efforts increased when Captain William Spaulding built a tote road leading northeast from the trail to his mining site south of Pine Lake. Although prospectors such as Mayhew and Spaulding and others did find traces of copper and silver here and elsewhere in the North Woods, they never struck it rich.

However, Mayhew was among the first to discover iron ore near Gunflint Lake. During the 1880s and 1890s, development of the Paulson Mine west of Gunflint Lake led to completion of a wagon road extending from the old Rove Lake trail. The Port Arthur, Duluth and Western Railroad, called the PeeDee, was constructed to get the iron ore to port and a boom town large enough to have a saloon and bawdy house sprang up on the shore of Gunflint Lake. However, neither the quantity nor the quality of ore could compete with the rich strikes further west on the Mesabi Range. The mine produced but one flatcar of ore before closing. Mine ownership changed hands several times during the following century, but the Paulson Mine has never paid off.

Exploring the BWCAW

The Boundary Waters Canoe Area Wilderness is the largest designated wilderness area in the eastern United States. A myriad of lakes, connected by streams and portage trails, dot the one-milllion-acre wilderness. Most of the area is closed to motorized use, so travel is predominately by canoe.

A permit system controls the number of visitors allowed in the BWCAW. A quota of permits is given to each of the many entry points to the wilderness. The permits, good for parties of up to ten people, are free. You can get them on a first-come, first-served basis at ranger stations or outfitters when you arrive, or you can reserve one in advance for your trip. Permit reservations cost five dollars and are recommended for anyone who doesn't like vacation surprises. You must pick up your permit in person upon arrival.

Travel is a combination of paddling and portaging. Novices should plan short, easy trips, but more experienced paddlers can venture into remote, rarely visited lakes. The BWCAW is bordered by the even larger Quetico Provincial Park wilderness in Ontario. Excellent maps of the entire canoe country are available. Bring them with you—you'll find no information kiosks in the woods.

Planning is essential for an enjoyable canoe trip. No cans and bottles are allowed in the BWCAW, so you must carry food and sundries in alternate containers. Don't plan to leave any trash in the wilderness. If you can't burn your garbage, carry it out with you. Practice packing before you go. Remember, the fewer trips across a portage, the better. Experienced canoers carry all their gear in one Duluth Pack.

Remember, too, that state regulations apply to the wilderness. You must have a Minnesota angling license if you plan to fish. Canoes must either be registered in your home state or have a Minnesota license. Everyone in your party must have a legal personal flotation device. Hunting is allowed in the BWCAW, with moose, black bear, and waterfowl the primary game, but you'll have little need to carry a firearm for protection in the BWCAW.

Although your party may be the only one on the lake, you must camp at designated campsites, which have pit toilets and fire rings. The campsites help lessen human impact on the fragile northern forest, limiting soil compaction, erosion, and pollution from human traffic to specific areas. An unwritten wilderness rule is to leave every camping area cleaner than you found it.

The BWCAW is a beautiful place, but it's not for everyone. You're on your own in the wilderness. There are no motel rooms, no hot dog stands. Biting insects, especially during June and July, can be enough to keep some folks away. You must also be prepared for the weather. May and September can be cold, and June is often dreary and cool. July and August have the warmest weather. You don't need permits in October, but weather then can vary from Indian summer to snow and ice.

Modern-day voyageurs consider these climatic extremes a challenge rather than a drawback. On cold, clear nights northern lights dance across the sky. Enduring a bug-ridden portage only makes success taste all the sweeter when you reach the other side. If the North Country were an easy place to live, it would have been settled and civilized long ago. Wild America still exists in places like the BWCAW. It's only a few paddlestrokes away.

Wilderness alternatives

Several excellent paddle and portage areas lie outside the BWCAW. These areas have no permit requirements, can and bottle restrictions, or motor bans. They are perfect for people who like the convenience of kicker outboard motors and canned goods, and some receive less use than much of the BWCAW.

Best known is the Timber-Frear area north of Schroeder. Despite recent road improvements, this area remains largely wild. A few miles to the south is Ninemile Lake, from which you can portage into Thunderbird and Shoepack lakes. Shoepack is so seldom visited that trees grow through the fire ring at the lake's only campsite.

Above Lutsen a canoe route runs from Crescent to Rice Lake. This route follows the headwaters of the Poplar River. Although downstream the Poplar supports brook trout, this area is best known for lots of small walleyes. East of the Gunflint Trail the Forest Service is developing campsites and portages on the "vegetable" lakes (so called because the lakes are named for vegetables).

Mountain Biking

For some folks, windshield tourism doesn't cut the mustard. They like to be able to feel the wind in their hair, smell the pines, get some exercise. For them, mountain biking is just the ticket, because the North Shore has an endless network of back roads and quiet trails. In fact, the North Shore probably has the best mountain biking in the Upper Midwest. The rugged topography of the Sawtooth Mountains provides ample opportunities to use every gear on the bike.

If you're new to the sport, don't let the ups and downs of the terrain scare you away. The variety of trails allows you to plan rides that match your skill level. If you have two vehicles, you can even set up a trip that's all downhill.

The best way to begin a North Shore mountain biking excursion is with a visit to a local bike shop or the Forest Service offices in Tofte and Grand Marais. There you'll find people knowledgeable about backcountry biking. They can suggest routes and provide maps. Be forewarned that no map shows every trail and tote road. A smart rider will carry the official Superior National Forest map, topographical maps, and a compass. Because you are following trails and roads, it's unlikely that you'll become lost.

Nevertheless, you can easily wind up in places where there is little or no traffic. Be prepared for emergencies. Before you leave, tell someone where you're going and when you plan to return. Carry food, water, insect repellent, and appropriate extra clothing.

It's especially important to carry a repair kit and know how to use it. Preventive maintenance will help you avoid breakdowns, so before you set out, check your drive train adjustments, lubrication, and tire pressure. The most common problem is flat tires, so know how to patch a puncture or repair a torn sidewall. You could also damage a derailleur or break a chain. A chain tool will allow you to make repairs so you can ride the bike out. Rough riding can loosen various nuts and bolts on your bike. Carry wrenches so you can tighten them.

What is the best riding season? Diehards hit the trails as soon as the snow melts, but casual riders should wait until the weather becomes consistently warm in mid-June. Good riding is available earlier, but you'll have to contend with mud and the first hatches of biting insects. Autumn riding is the most scenic, but it's also the busiest time of year in the woods. You'll share the roads with hordes of leaf lookers and grouse hunters. Throughout the season you may encounter logging trucks.

How do you choose a route? Adventurous riders can just

jump on a bike and start pedaling. Every back road leads somewhere. Less confident riders can follow loops that the Forest Service has marked with signs. Routes range from wide gravel roads to pothole-infested tote roads. The most difficult riding is on snowmobile and cross-country ski trails, because they have no roadbed. High grass can be a problem on lesser-used trails during the summer. No matter where you ride, wear a helmet to prevent head injuries. The only places that are off-limits to bikers are the Grand Portage Trail, the BWCAW, and the Superior Hiking Trail.

A scenic ride for beginners, the Mark Lake–Mississippi Creek loop north of Pike Lake, follows logging roads and a short stretch of improved gravel roadway. Forest Service signs mark a portion of the route. A more difficult excursion is the climb from Highway 61 on the Hall Road east of Lutsen. You can follow old roads around the north side of Deeryard Lake and eventually go back downhill to the highway on the Cascade ski trail system.

Just because you don't own a mountain bike doesn't mean you can't join the fun. Mountain bike rentals are available at various locations along the North Shore. Renting a bike is the best way for a beginner to be introduced to the sport.

Chippewa City

MILEPOST 110 Racial and class segregation was long a matter of course on the North Shore. During the fur-trading days the Indians and voyageurs were required to camp outside the stockade at Grand Portage, while inside the wealthy company partners (and no doubt some "lucky" Indian women) lived in comparative elegance. Early accounts often mention Indian encampments near white settlements.

Chippewa City developed on the eastern outskirts of Grand Marais as Indian families gradually gave up their nomadic lifestyle during the 1800s. For years, in fact, it *was*

Grand Marais, because so few white settlers lived in the community. Indians and whites apparently got along well. A number of Indians figure prominently in local history, and white men married Indian women.

Chippewa City existed as a community into the twentieth century. Today the shacks of impoverished Indians have disappeared. A small cemetery and the St. Francis Xavier Church, which was built in 1895, remain. You can see the church on the lake side of Highway 61 east of Grand Marais, and a sign tells its history. Catholic services are occasionally held there.

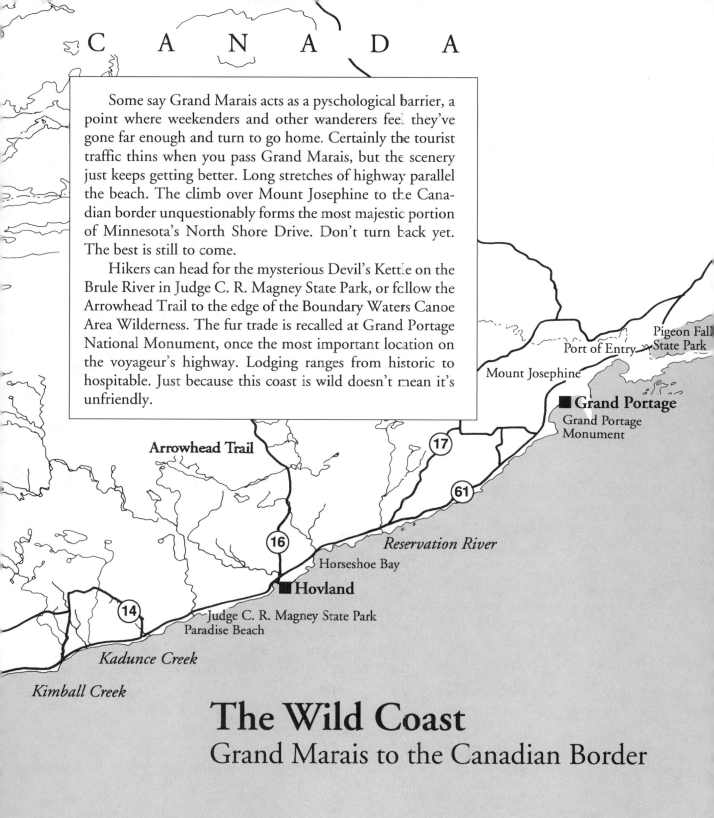

Some say Grand Marais acts as a pyschological barrier, a point where weekenders and other wanderers feel they've gone far enough and turn to go home. Certainly the tourist traffic thins when you pass Grand Marais, but the scenery just keeps getting better. Long stretches of highway parallel the beach. The climb over Mount Josephine to the Canadian border unquestionably forms the most majestic portion of Minnesota's North Shore Drive. Don't turn back yet. The best is still to come.

Hikers can head for the mysterious Devil's Kettle on the Brule River in Judge C. R. Magney State Park, or follow the Arrowhead Trail to the edge of the Boundary Waters Canoe Area Wilderness. The fur trade is recalled at Grand Portage National Monument, once the most important location on the voyageur's highway. Lodging ranges from historic to hospitable. Just because this coast is wild doesn't mean it's unfriendly.

The Wild Coast
Grand Marais to the Canadian Border

Kimball Creek

MILEPOST 117 Keep going. There's no place to park here, and the mouth of Kimball Creek is private, anyway. Kimball Creek is named for Charles Kimball, a geological survey crew member who drowned near here in the summer of 1864.

A century later, during the early 1960s, the Minnesota Department of Natural Resources (DNR) did a fisheries survey of Kimball Creek in conjunction with a steelhead study. In this tiny stream biologists found a stunning diversity of fish species: rainbow trout, brook trout, brown trout, sea lamprey, northern redbelly dace, finescale dace, flathead minnow, blacknose dace, longnose dace, creek chub, pearl dace, longnose sucker, burbot, brook stickleback, walleye, mottled sculpin, and slimy sculpin.

Rainbow trout, actually juvenile steelhead, made up the bulk of the fish population and numbered in the thousands. However, the chance of an individual fish reaching adulthood was slim. The number of adult spawners that ascended the stream each spring averaged less than one hundred. Researchers captured the returning spawners in a weir near the river mouth, marked them, and released the fish to continue upstream. They also trapped surviving fish after they had spawned, as they migrated back to the lake. Although the steelhead spent an average of 10.5 days in the stream, the time that individual fish remained varied from a few hours to more than a month.

A higher proportion of females than males survived the spawn, leading the biologists to theorize that the males were more stressed by the rigors of spawning, more susceptible to fishing, or both.

Colvill

MILEPOST 117 If you're ever out driving the backroads of Colvill on a quiet evening, stop at the intersection of the Trout Lake Road and County 14. Turn off the ignition, roll down the window, and listen. The barks and howls you hear in the distance come from sled dogs. Living here in what can only be called Outer Colvill is an enclave of dog mushers. Two things brought them here, an abundance of snowy trails and an absence of neighbors. Some folks frown on having a kennel of sixty dogs next door.

Mushing is a way of life, not a hobby. Feeding and caring for dozens of dogs occupies a portion of every day year-round. Autumn and winter are devoted to training teams and racing. It's difficult for a musher to find time for vacations or to hold a "real" job. Yet maintaining a kennel of competitive sled dogs is expensive, easily costing ten thousand dollars or more each year. That money has to come from somewhere. Some mushers work at part-time or seasonal jobs. Others depend on sponsors. Still others have found ways to make mushing pay for itself—giving sled rides to tourists or manufacturing dogsledding equipment. Rare is the dog driver who is rolling in the dough.

Why do they it? To answer that question you have to step on a sled and follow the dogs for a few miles down a snowy trail. But be careful. You may like it so much that before you know it you'll be living in a shack in the woods surrounded by sixty barking dogs.

Kadunce Creek

MILEPOST 118 The sign on the highway is wrong. It labels this small, clear-running stream as Kodonce Creek. The proper spelling is Kadunce.

Actually, the stream has an earlier, less-appealing name—Diarrhea River—that dates back to the 1850s. Apparently, at least one explorer suffered some unpleasantness, which he blamed on the drinking water.

Don't let the name stop you from enjoying this place. A parking lot on the east side of the stream is just a few feet from the beach. Here you'll find one of the best collections of flat skipping stones along the North Shore. Please, however, don't throw rocks in the water if someone is fishing there. The splashing from the rocks and the commotion you make on the beach will frighten the wary trout. If the angler was there first, let him or her cast in peace.

Across the highway from the parking area a spur trail follows the creek to the Superior Hiking Trail. It's a pleasant hike and, aside from one steep hill, relatively easy. As you start walking upstream you'll notice that logs have been placed in the stream to create small waterfalls. These structures, called Hewlitt ramps, improve the stream habitat for trout and other fish. Without them, the creek would be little more than a cobblestone gutter, with few pools where fish could live. The Kadunce receives a run of steelhead in the spring, and the pools people have created provide these fish with places to rest and hide while they spawn. Baby steelhead and brook trout use the pools throughout the year. If you look carefully into the water, you'll see tiny fish darting about. Those are baby trout.

Because it is so easily accessible, the Kadunce is one of the most heavily fished steelhead streams along the North Shore. For this reason, trout anglers should practice catch-and-release here. The trout you let go not only will provide sport for another angler but also will be able to spawn and renew the cycle of life. Wild trout are one of the North Shore's finest treasures.

As you follow the trail upstream you'll soon reach a point where it leaves the river and climbs a steep bank. Actually, it's leading you up to the rim of the canyon. The Kadunce flows through a short but remarkable red rhyolite canyon that is like a miniature model of the Devil Track. In places, the canyon drops to dizzying depths but is so narrow you could almost jump across. Keep an eye on the kids.

There are no handrails here. Hopefully there never will be, because they'd serve no other purpose than to remove the wild from this exceptionally beautiful place.

Can you drink the water?

One can only speculate about the ailment that led an early explorer to dub this stream "Diarrhea Creek." Even though the water in this and many North Shore streams appears clean and clear, drinking it is unwise. You can never be certain what lies upstream. This is wild country, but it is not unsettled. Perhaps upstream the creek flows through a pasture or, more likely, receives effluent from septic systems.

Another concern is an illness called giardiasis, or beaver fever, caused by *Giardia lamblia*. This troublesome bacteria is often associated with beavers, and rare is the North Shore stream that isn't impounded by a series of beaver dams. Giardiasis, although not fatal, is a knock-down, drag-out illness that can leave you subsisting on a Jell-O diet. No one who has had it ever wants to get it again.

Be smart. Carry a supply of drinking water. Otherwise, boil or treat stream and lake water before drinking it.

MILEPOST 122 Just past the intersection with County Road 14 (locally known as the East Colvill Road) you'll see a yellow sign that says Moose Area. The next mile or so affords the best place along Highway 61 to see one of these black beasts, especially near the small pond on the lake side of the road. Just past the pond the highway touches Paradise Beach.

Nothing marks the spot, just a couple of rough pull-offs. You'll find no picnic tables, fire grates, or hiking trails— nothing but a beautiful fine-gravel beach. In the summer, the seagulls that nest offshore on the rocky Marr Islands frequent the beach. Occasionally, a flock of Canada geese waddles across the gravel. During the winter you can see

Paradise Beach

hardy goldeneye ducks and, farther out, old-squaw. When the bay is frozen, you may even see coyotes or timber wolves crossing the ice.

Regardless of the season, the attraction of Paradise Beach is its wildness. Here you can sense the vastness of the lake and the boreal forest, both just a few steps from your car. It is a good place to stop and listen to the talking ice on a below-zero winter morning or to push out a canoe on a quiet summer evening.

Photographers should visit Paradise Beach at sunrise, when cold lake mists weave among the shoreline spruces. If you are lucky, you may hear wolves howling on the hillside above the highway. In country where natural beauty is commonplace, Paradise Beach stands out.

How to Watch a Wolf

Chance encounters with timber wolves can occur at any time of year. However, if you really want to see a North Shore wolf, the best time is late winter, for a couple of reasons. First, the deep snows concentrate wintering deer, and the wolves that prey on them, in a narrow band along the Lake Superior shoreline. Here the deer find less snow, a somewhat warmer climate, and food. The DNR manages the forests within the deer yards to supply the animals with browse, and many North Shore residents feed the deer. The other reason is that Lake Superior freezes over in February and March, and the wolves use the ice as a travel route.

This doesn't mean you'll run out of film taking pictures of wolves, but it does give you about the best chance in Minnesota to see a wolf in the wild. Wildlife watching carries no guarantees, but being in the right place at the right time certainly ups your odds. Just remember, the open expanse of Lake Superior usually doesn't form ice until late February.

Potential wolf watchers should plan to be out at dawn, because the predators are most likely to be seen then. At the very least, you'll be treated to a sunrise over Lake Superior. Dress warmly, wear boots, and carry a pair of binoculars. Then walk down to areas of shoreline that aren't visible from the highway. A good place to begin your search is near any of the state parks, all of which support wintering deer herds. Wolf sightings are commonly reported from Lutsen to the Canadian border.

Wolves use the ice to their advantage when hunting. They travel along the shoreline to sneak up on a deer, then drive the unfortunate whitetail out on the ice to kill it. Sometimes you'll see a flock of ravens offshore near some bloodstained snow, feeding on what the wolves have left. On occasion, motorists on Highway 61 have actually seen wolves take down a deer. The large canines may even be seen in the highway ditch, especially at night, feeding on roadkills.

Once wolves are spotted in a particular area, they may remain in the vicinity for a day or longer. For whatever reason—probably because they are difficult to approach unseen—wolves seem to be less cautious when they are on the ice. They have even been known to walk past the Grand Marais harbor.

Not every canine you see on the ice will be a wolf. The North Shore also has populations of red fox and coyotes. Red fox are easily identified by their coloration and small size. Coyotes are larger—like a medium-sized dog—but still much smaller than a full grown timber wolf. Coyotes also have a pointed snout. They are seen throughout the year by early morning and evening North Shore travelers.

If you don't see a wolf, you should at least be able to find their tracks. You may see tracks on the frozen lake (be careful, the ice may be treacherously thin) or on cross-country ski trails, especially those wending through the deer yards. Ask locals where you might see wolves or their tracks. They'll get you pointed in the right direction.

Judge C. R. Magney State Park

MILEPOST 124 An old steelhead fisherman likes to tell of the time he fell into the Brule River beneath the footbridge in Judge C. R. Magney State Park. Down he tumbled through the high-water rapids, eventually washing into a pool where another man was fishing.

"See any fish on your way through?" the man asked.

We owe this state park and ten other parks and waysides to the hard work of another fisherman, Clarence Magney, a Minnesota Supreme Court justice and Duluth mayor, who died in 1962. The Brule River was reputed to be one of his favorite places to fish.

The Brule River, one of the North Shore's mightiest, forms the centerpiece of this park. Not far upstream from Highway 61 it flows through a deep canyon, where angry currents rumble over rock ledges. Two of these ledges, Lower Falls and Upper Falls, both about a mile up from the highway, are impressive waterfalls. Sometimes in the spring and fall you can see trout and salmon leaping Lower Falls.

Park visitors walk the uphill and sometimes muddy path on the river's east bank for more than these two beautiful waterfalls. The main attraction is one of the North Shore's more puzzling natural wonders, the Devil's Kettle. Just upstream from Upper Falls a portion of the river disappears into a hole in the rocks. To the best of anyone's knowledge, it never reappears. Local legends say dye, Ping-Pong balls, logs, and even a car have been dropped into the Devil's Kettle and not seen again. (How anyone could get an automobile to such a remote spot is open to conjecture.) The round-trip hike to Devil's Kettle takes about an hour. The best time to see the Kettle is when the water is low; in high water it's difficult to discern.

During the Depression, prior to the area's becoming a state park, the west bank of the Brule River held a work camp. Unemployed young men went to work here logging, farming, and building fire roads. The crews built a small tourist park along the river and established a sawmill inland to salvage timber destroyed in a disastrous 1936 fire. Concrete foundations from the camp are still visible in the park's thirty-six-site rustic campground.

Magney may be the North Shore's wildest park. The park holdings include more than four thousand acres and extend about five miles inland, but east of the river no official trail goes beyond the Devil's Kettle. On the west side a two-plus-mile trail leads to a shelter atop a bluff overlooking the river. Continue bushwhacking about three miles further upriver and you'll reach another waterfall.

A loop off the trail on the west side of the river follows Gauthier Creek, a tributary of the Brule, for about a half mile. The DNR has done some stream improvement along this stretch to create pools for baby steelhead. Another loop trail on the west side of the river leads—via an unmarked anglers' spur trail—to the mouth of Gauthier Creek at the base of Lower falls. In the spring, steelhead ascend Gauthier about a quarter mile till stopped by a plunging waterfall. If you are quiet, you can follow a path on the bank and see spawning steelhead in the stream. The DNR is considering closing this portion of the stream to fishing because the fish are so vulnerable to anglers. In order to reach the Gauthier Creek waterfall, you'll have to cross the creek. Wear at least knee-high rubber boots or plan to get wet. Please, don't try the newest West Coast sport—crickin—which is simply sloshing up the middle of a small stream. Every step you take could crush dozens of trout eggs and fry.

In the spring, when water conditions are right, whitewater kayakers descend the Brule. However, this is not a sport for the thrill-seeking novice. The kayakers launch several miles upstream and portage unnavigable stretches, such as the Devil's Kettle area. If you want to test your mettle against the river's might, go with someone who is familiar with the Brule. Anglers should also exercise caution when wading the Brule or exploring the canyon.

While we're on the subject of do's and don'ts, here's another. Leave wildflowers where you find them. Magney's floral display begins in the spring and continues through the warm months. Along the hiking trails you can find everything from marsh marigolds to jack-in-the-pulpits. Lots of coral roots, a variety of orchid, and species such as clintonia and twinflower grow here. In the canyons you may discover uncommon plant communities that thrive in the cool, moist environment.

Magney supports a variety of wildlife. White-tailed deer and coyotes are common sights, especially during the winter. Mergansers, mink, and mallards can be seen on the river. Less visible residents of the park include timber wolves, moose, pine marten, fisher, and otter. Prior to the construction of a large parking lot, spring visitors were treated to the evening aerial displays of mating woodcock above a small wetlands adjacent to the campground. Now potential woodcock watchers must do some hiking in order to locate the haunts of these long-billed birds.

The construction of the parking lot also brought another change to the park. The small lot along Highway 61 on the east side of the river, where hikers and anglers could park without buying a state-park sticker, has been closed. Now you must either enter the park or leave your vehicle on the shoulder of the highway.

Naniboujou Lodge

MILEPOST 124 You'll see few serpents along the North Shore aside from an occasional garter snake. Prior to road construction and the clearing of the land, which created habitat, they were rarer still. According to Indian legend the devil let loose no-see-ums here, but the god Naniboujou chased him away before he could unload his parcel of snakes. At least that's what it says in the original promotional brochure for the Naniboujou Club.

The twenties were still roaring when the club opened in

July 1929. It was a grand event, still the largest gathering ever in Cook County. The new club was to be a getaway for the nation's elite; members included such worthies as Jack Dempsey, Babe Ruth, and Ring Lardner. Whether or not Dempsey or Ruth ever visited Naniboujou is uncertain, but local legend has it that Clark Gable once stayed there. Club bylaws stipulated that no more than 25 percent of the members could be Minnesota residents and any two board members could vote down a potential member.

The scale of the club's plans sounds impressive even today. Naniboujou included a half mile of Lake Superior shoreline on each side of the Brule River, as well as thirty-three hundred acres that included much of the present Judge C. R. Magney State Park. A dock for the steamer *America* extended into the lake, and members could also reach the club via the newly completed North Shore Road. The lodge was complete when the club opened, and riding stables, tennis courts, and cottages, as well as a plush hunting lodge inland near the Canadian border, were planned.

Unfortunately, the stock market crashed in October. The Duluth businessmen who built Naniboujou knew the club needed one thousand members to survive, but they were only able to attract half of that number. Perhaps the membership fee of $175 and the $25 annual dues were too expensive for the Depression era. The club's mortgage was foreclosed during the early 1930s, and a hotel chain acquired the property. The lodge continued to cater to an exclusive clientele until it closed during World War II. Following the war it was purchased by the Hussey family, who reopened the lodge and operated it until selling it to the Wallaces in 1961. The Wallaces sold Naniboujou in 1980. Present owners Tim and Nancy Ramey managed the facility for a couple of years before purchasing it.

Naniboujou Lodge has remained much the same since 1929, which is why it is on the National Register of Historic Places. The original cypress siding still covers the exterior.

Step inside and you return to an era of elegance. The dining room is striking. The walls and ceiling were painted in a colorful Cree Indian motif by artist Antione Gouffe. Hanging from the ceiling are exquisite paper chandeliers, which may have been prototypes for bronze or Tiffany chandeliers that were never built. A massive fireplace, built of two hundred tons of native rock gathered on the beach, separates the dining room and kitchen. Only the solarium on the lakeside wall has been added since the lodge first opened. It covers what was once a shuffleboard court.

Hovland

MILEPOST 128 Your first glimpse of Hovland when approaching from the west shows you houses nestled at the foot of an immense, forested hill. Sometimes mist weaves through the treetops. At other times the balsams stand like noble soldiers in snowy uniforms. It is but a momentary image as you crest the hill—if you're not watching, you'll miss it.

One could say the same of Hovland itself. There are no stores, no gas stations, and no plush resorts. The only going concern is the post office.

It wasn't always this way. Once this little community on Chicago Bay thrived, with stores, a school, and places to stay. Indeed, Hovland was among the earliest tourist destinations on the North Shore. Fishing was so good the town was billed as the Lake Trout Capital of the World. Here, on May 30, 1955, G. H. Nelson came to shore with a forty-three-pound, eight-ounce lake trout, which remains the state record.

The lunker lake trout are gone, but there still is good fishing off Hovland. Once home port of commercial lake trout and herring fishermen, Hovland is now a launching point for sport anglers. A visit to the Hovland dock will give you a rewarding look at its past. The first deepwater dock was built shortly after the turn of the century in response to increasing steamboat traffic. The timber-rich country to the north was being logged and Chicago Bay bustled with activity. At the foot of the dock stands a large bell that was rung when ships arrived.

Near the dock you can see fish houses, other remnants from Hovland's past. Now only a minimal amount of commercial fishing takes place here. But come here at dawn when the lake is calm and misty, and it takes little imagination to envision Norwegian fishermen pushing off in their cedar skiffs.

Today you might wonder what Hovland residents do for a living. Since the town has no visible economy, it's a fair question. What Hovland does have is a population best described as eclectic. Some were attracted here by the area's remoteness. Others were born here and decided there was no place better. Some are loggers or sawyers. Some hold government jobs. A few work in Grand Marais. Others are retired.

As one former resident said, "Hovland is a community of good people working hard and getting by."

How the locals say it

The way you pronounce "Hovland" is an immediate indication to locals of how long you've been there. Most strangers say it as it's spelled, rhyming with "loveland." Residents say it with a long O. In fact, some early accounts actually spelled the name "Hoveland."

The town was named by pioneer Anna Brunes after her grandfather's estate in Norway. The first settlers, Ole Brunes and Nels Ludwig Eliasen, homesteaded at the mouth of the Flute Reed River in 1888. In 1988, the community commemorated the foresight and perseverance of its first residents with a centennial celebration.

A fisherman's ordeal

On Wednesday, the eve of Thanksgiving, 1958, Hovland commercial fisherman Helmer Aakvik realized that fellow fisherman Carl Hammer had gone out early that morning and not returned. A strong nor'wester was blowing, so Aakvik went out to look for him.

The Coast Guard was alerted to Hammer's disappearance by midmorning and brought a small boat to Hovland to search for the now two missing men. An Air Force jet and another fisherman also joined the search. The weather was so cold the gas lines froze on the Coast Guard boat and the crew returned to Grand Marais for a larger, more seaworthy craft. November is a particularly vicious month on Lake Superior, and this day was no exception. The seas were running ten to fifteen feet and the temperature was just fourteen degrees above zero.

The Coast Guard returned to Hovland, but was unable to locate the fishermen. The weight of the ice that formed on the Coast Guard boat caused the craft to ride six to eight inches lower in the water. Finally, darkness brought an end to the search. Winds increased to forty-four miles per hour and the temperature dropped to near zero. Little hope was held that the lost men would survive. However, the Coast Guard cutter *Woodrush,* called in from Isle Royale, kept looking through the night.

The next day the search continued. Complicating efforts a steamlike mist rose above the water. Visibility was as little as sixty yards. If the Coast Guard crew had relaxed their vigilance for but a moment, they might not have seen Aakvik's small boat bobbing in the mist. Aakvik didn't know the Coast Guard was near until the two vessels bumped together. Even his face was covered with ice.

Once ashore, Aakvik's first request was for a chew of snuff. Aside from frostbitten toes and swollen hands, he was none the worse for his twenty-four-hour ordeal. Certainly,

Aakvik's inherent Scandinavian toughness and his fisherman's savvy were the reasons he survived. He had almost reached shore the first night when he ran out of gasoline. Eventually, he tossed his two outboard motors overboard to lighten his ice-laden boat. Every moment was occupied with rowing and chipping ice from the craft. When found, he was six miles offshore.

When he told news reporters his story, he also mentioned the beauty of the waves and spray in the moonlight. Even battling for his life, Aakvik still appreciated the wonder of the lake. Such is the stuff of legend. Carl Hammer, however, was never found.

The Arrowhead Trail

MILEPOST 128 The Arrowhead Trail leads eighteen miles north from Hovland to McFarland Lake on the edge of the BWCAW. It is paved for two miles or so to the top of the hill; from there on it is a wide gravel road. The road was renamed "Arrowhead Trail" in the interest of tourism. Oldtimers still refer to it as the McFarland Road in deference to John McFarland, a prospector and settler who, in the 1890s, built the road through trackless wilderness.

The wild, rugged country the trail traverses is included in the Grand Portage State Forest. This area has no lakeside resorts or manicured ski trail systems, just lakes, streams, and trees. A network of forest roads will take you to lakes stocked with walleyes and trout. Along the way you may see moose, bear, and grouse.

Paddle a canoe on Swamp River for an excellent and out-of-the-way place to do some wildlife watching. A small dam along the Otter Lake Road (about ten miles up the trail) has created an extensive wetlands. Here you can see many species of ducks, raptors, and other marshland birds. Early and late in the day you are likely to see moose. The river is loaded with hammer-handle-sized northern pike, which makes it a great place to take kids fishing. You can reach Swamp River from the Otter Lake Road or from an access road off the Arrowhead Trail near its junction with the Irish Creek Road.

Twelve miles up the trail you'll see a small sign designating an overlook on the east side of the road. Here you have a magnificent view of Portage Brook valley. Just beyond the far ridges lie South Fowl Lake, the Pigeon River, and the Canadian border. Portions of the valley have been clear-cut. If you look closely in these openings you may see moose or bear. The new growth in the clear-cuts provides food for these large animals.

Less than a mile farther north a forest road leads westward to the Gunflint Trail. Stop here and get out. If you look closely on the east side of the trail you'll find a small, unmarked footpath. A short walk will take you to a beautiful, hidden waterfall on Portage Brook.

At McFarland Lake you'll find one of the few swimming beaches in Cook County. The beach is shallow and sandy, and you can wade out some distance without getting wet above the waist. The only drawback is that the beach also serves as a boat launch area, although it is rarely, if ever, crowded. McFarland, which is a popular entry point into the BWCAW, also has a boat access.

On your way back down the trail you can take a short loop route and look for wildlife. Go east on the Otter Lake Road about six miles until you reach the Jackson Lake Road. Turn south (the only direction you can turn) and follow the Jackson Lake Road about eight miles back to the Arrowhead Trail. The entire route is gravel, but there are no other side roads, so it's tough to get lost. If you keep going straight on the Otter Lake Road you'll go through the Grand Portage Indian Reservation. The maple ridges on the reservation are beautiful during the fall. The road through the reservation is passable for automobiles, but is more suitable for trucks.

Return of the Natives

Dramatic changes have occurred beneath Superior's waves during the past century. One hundred years ago, commercial fishing came into its own as a North Shore industry. Improvements in transportation made it possible to ship fish to more distant markets. Herring, lake trout, and whitefish dominated the catch. Back then, fishermen no doubt thought Superior's abundant fish stocks would last forever, but with the taming of the North Shore came change.

On land, large-scale logging dramatically altered tributary streams. Water levels were manipulated for log drives with dams and other control devices. The huge logs chased each other down the rivers, gouging out the stream channels like bulldozers. This action, coupled with erosion of the denuded landscape, resulted in a buildup of gravel deposits at the river mouths, which destroyed productive estuary areas. Stripped of vegetation that provided shade, logged-over streams warmed during the hot days of summer.

In the water, sawdust and other industrial waste smothered spawning areas and added an array of pollutants to the ecosystem. Overfishing also damaged fish populations. Both lake trout and herring were often netted when they were concentrated in spawning areas. Fisheries historians have traced a link between netting in spawning areas and the depletion of local herring stocks along the North Shore.

However, the coup de grace for native trout and herring was the introduction into Lake Superior of two saltwater species: the rainbow smelt and the sea lamprey. The smelt swam into Lake Superior on its own following its introduction to a lake in the Lake Michigan drainage. At first it was thought that smelt would provide an additional source of food for lake trout. That they did, but they also preyed upon baby herring and whitefish—decimating stocks of both. The lamprey followed the system of locks and canals through the Great Lakes. An eel-like fish parasite, the sea lamprey uses its rasping, sucker-shaped mouth to attach to the flanks of a living soft-skinned fish such as trout, and then sucks the juices from its body.

The lamprey was first discovered in Lake Superior in 1946. Within just a few years it was apparent that lake-trout stocks, as well as populations of other soft-skinned fish such as burbot, were in trouble. When the international Great Lakes Fisheries Commission started chemical lamprey control in 1958, Superior had virtually become a dead sea. The control program didn't eradicate lampreys, but has kept them in check. Lakewide, lamprey numbers are now about 10 percent of their 1960's peak. Although they still destroy large numbers of lake trout and other fish, lamprey control allows fisheries managers to work toward restoring Lake Superior's fishery.

Lake Superior was the only Great Lake in which lake trout were not completely wiped out. Through research and interviews with commercial fishermen, biologists learned where and when lake trout had once spawned. Many strains of lake trout, which had different spawning times and physical characteristics, had populated the lake. Today, the two best-known strains are the redfin and the siscowet. The redfin is a lean, firm-fleshed trout prized by anglers. The siscowet is a deepwater trout with large deposits of body fat.

In some places, such as Isle Royale, healthy stocks of wild lake trout still reproduce. However, along the Minnesota coast natural reproduction accounts for 20 percent or less of the lake trout population. About 350,000 lake trout, most of them raised in the federal hatchery system, are stocked in the Minnesota waters of Lake Superior each year. There is continued hope that stocked fish will use the historic spawning areas and the wild population will grow. However, the hatchery trout have a different genetic makeup than the native fish, so their internal clocks and compasses may not guide them to the spawning areas. Luck as much as anything else may play a role in the spawning success of stocked fish.

Together, stocked and wild lake trout provide a valuable North Shore resource. Assessment nettings that commercial fishermen conduct in spring and fall for the Minnesota DNR monitor the trout population. Participants are allowed a quota of trout that they can catch and sell. They check the trout for lamprey scars or for clipped fins, which indicate that they were born in a hatchery.

Lake herring, one of several species of cisco found in Superior, have rebounded in recent years as smelt numbers declined. No one is quite sure what caused this change in the lake's forage base, but it could be that trout and salmon stocked in the lake may have preyed heavily upon smelt, giving the herring population a chance to increase. The herring recovery could spell good news for lake trout, because the silvery fish were their original food source. Perhaps the huge lake trout for which Superior was once famous will return. However, it takes years for lake trout to grow to trophy sizes, and lamprey go after larger fish. So, even though Lake Superior's fishery has made a dramatic recovery, we can't take fish dinners for granted. Instead, we should credit fisheries managers for their success and urge them to keep up the hard work.

Horseshoe Bay

MILEPOST 130 About a mile beyond Hovland you'll see a small sign marking a boat access to the lake. All you'll find there is a small parking area and a rather steep boat ramp, but Horseshoe Bay is a lovely place. The deep inlet is somewhat protected from the lake's stormy wrath and the wild shoreline conjures images of a pristine Superior.

Someday, all of that may change. Horseshoe Bay has been identified as a potential harbor of refuge. For an estimated cost of five million dollars, nine hundred feet of breakwalls could be built to enclose the bay, where docks for up to twenty-five boats and additional launch ramps would be constructed. Horseshoe Bay could then be a convenient launch area for boaters headed to Isle Royale.

Reservation River

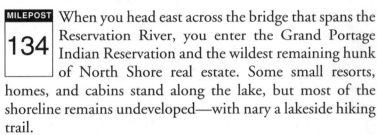 When you head east across the bridge that spans the Reservation River, you enter the Grand Portage Indian Reservation and the wildest remaining hunk of North Shore real estate. Some small resorts, homes, and cabins stand along the lake, but most of the shoreline remains undeveloped—with nary a lakeside hiking trail.

Two routes lead from here to the community of Grand Portage. The first route follows the highway. An enchanting view of a fisherman's home can be seen from one of its scenic pull-offs. The second route is along Cook County 17, which loops inland from the highway just east of the Reservation River and meets it again just west of Grand Portage. This road was once the highway, and you'll pass what may be the most ancient billboard in the state. At the ghost town of Mineral Center you can turn north and follow a decent gravel road to the old border crossing on the Pigeon River. Along the way you'll pass the trailhead for the Grand Portage ski trail system and the historic Grand Portage Trail.

The Grand Portage Band regulates hunting and fishing on Indian lands. You must have hunting and fishing permits issued by the band, which are available in Grand Portage. Some reservation seasons differ from state seasons, so be sure you know the regulations. Campers should also check regulations prior to pitching a tent.

Grand Portage

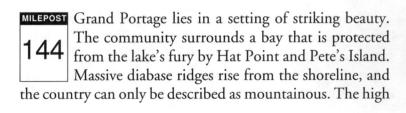 Grand Portage lies in a setting of striking beauty. The community surrounds a bay that is protected from the lake's fury by Hat Point and Pete's Island. Massive diabase ridges rise from the shoreline, and the country can only be described as mountainous. The high

peaks have names like Mount Rose, Mount Josephine, and Mount Maud.

Grand Portage is the Minnesota North Shore's only Ojibwa community. Indian people have been living here since before the coming of the fur traders. Here you can find people who still live off the land: hunting moose, trapping, and fishing in the big lake. Inquire locally and you can purchase both fresh and smoked fish, as well as locally made beadwork.

For visitors, the focal point of the community is Grand Portage Lodge and Casino. The facility, operated by the Grand Portage Band, was built in the 1970s and has undergone rapid expansion since the addition of the casino in 1990. Regardless of whether you plan to gamble, it's a good place to get information about local attractions. Guided tours to the Witch Tree (the only way to see it now) are arranged through the lodge. You can also get information about the Grand Portage Ski Trail system, which has been in operation since 1975.

Two marina facilities operate on Grand Portage Bay, a popular starting point for boaters headed to Isle Royale. The crossing to the island is about twenty miles. Daily ferry service to Isle Royale departs from Grand Portage during the summer.

The Grand Portage coast has plenty for you to explore, including the Susie Islands and Wauswaugoning Bay. Anglers find good fishing for lake trout and salmon off both Grand Portage and Isle Royale, and charter services are available.

Grand Portage also has the distinction of having the only log school building in Minnesota. It's located a quarter mile east of Grand Portage National Monument. Students attend kindergarten through sixth grade there, and then are bused to Grand Marais for junior high and high school.

The Witch Tree

The weatherworn cedar stands alone on the rocky shore of Hat Point. Its roots grip the rock like aged fingers, drawing sustenance from an invisible source. It grows so close to the water that you can only wonder how it has been able to withstand the lake's ferocity. Yet it has done so for at least four hundred years.

The Indians call this tree Spirit Little Cedar. For centuries they left tobacco offerings at its base for safe passage on Lake Superior, especially for making the precarious crossing to Isle Royale. The French voyageurs followed the tradition. Even today you can find broken cigarettes and sprinkled tobacco around the roots.

During the twentieth century this small but ancient cedar began to attract artists. One of them, Dewey Albinson, coined the name Witch Tree because of the tree's gnarled appearance. The name has no connection to the one given to it by the Indians.

During the 1980s the privately owned Witch Tree property was put up for sale. A local fund-raising committee was formed to purchase the property for the Grand Portage Band. The sale was completed in 1989. Unfortunately, publicity generated by the fund-raising campaign spurred an enormous boost in visitors to the tree. The small woodland path leading to the tree soon became a thoroughfare. Concerned about the impact the increased traffic was having on the tree site, the band closed the site to the public in 1991. Guided tours are now available through Grand Portage Lodge.

Rendezvous Days

During the fur-trading years, Grand Portage came alive for a short time each summer during a celebration called the rendezvous. Voyageurs and traders from the western trading posts met their counterparts from Montreal to exchange furs and trade goods. This get together followed months of isolation so a good time was had by all. Then the heavily laden canoes would depart in two directions: back to Montreal with the year's supply of furs and inland to the traders' winter camps.

Each summer the fur-trade era is remembered during Rendezvous Days, held on the second weekend in August. The event is a joint effort of the National Park Service and the local community. There's nothing else quite like it along the North Shore.

Along the lakeshore near the stockade modern-day voyageurs set up camp. Amid the teepees you'll find men and women dressed in clothing of the era, making paddles, cooking in iron kettles, and working on other crafts. On the powwow grounds over the hill, drums are beaten and merchants sell everything from furs to fry bread. Be sure to try the mooseburgers.

Gateway to the West

As hiking trails go, it isn't much. The pathway is muddy and not particularly scenic. When you reach the northern end of the nine-mile trail, you must turn around and go back the way you came. Perhaps that's why only two hundred to three hundred persons among the forty thousand who visit Grand Portage National Monument annually actually hike the historic trail.

Yet those few adventurous hikers, curious historians, and border-route canoeists have the privilege of walking one of Minnesota's oldest highways, an overland crossing that was key to European westward expansion. From here, explorers and traders ventured all the way to the Canadian Rockies. From here, wealthy Europeans pillaged the wildlife resources of a continent and began the destruction of native cultures. For twenty-five years Grand Portage was a key link in the lucrative fur-trade industry.

The portage predates the fur trade, probably by centuries. Below Fort Charlotte, at the northern end of the portage, the Pigeon River brawls through a twenty-two-mile, tortured course of rapids, waterfalls, gorges, and shallow riffles. Passage by canoe to the river's mouth at Lake Superior was impossible. The only alternative was to leave the river at this point, shoulder canoes and their cargoes, and portage nearly nine miles to the lake. The route was no cakewalk, but the seven-hundred-foot descent from the river to the lake was relatively gradual, considering the imposing hills that rise up on either side of the trail. The portage ended on the beach at Grand Portage Bay, a sheltered natural harbor. Grand Portage, which the Indians knew as the Great Carrying Place, was not the only passage inland. The St. Louis River, entering the lake at Duluth, and the Kamanistiqua River flowing into Thunder Bay were also traveled by aboriginal canoers. Both routes had arduous portages.

The first Europeans to arrive at Lake Superior were the French. Etienne Brulé came up the St. Mary's River from Lake Huron in 1622 and may have traveled as far as Grand Portage. However, the first Frenchman known to use the portage was Pierre Gaultier de Varennes, Sieur de La Vérendrye, in 1731. Upon learning the length of the portage his men mutinied and refused to cross it. A party of volunteers led by La Vérendrye's nephew went over the portage and continued inland to Rainy Lake, where they established a trading post.

Apparently the French adapted to northern life. They learned from the native people how to survive and adopted some of their ways and customs. One skill the French acquired from the Indians was use of the canoe. French paddlers became a class of men romanticized today, the voyageurs.

The British placed Grand Portage on the historical map when they established the inland headquarters of the Northwest Company in 1779. Unlike the French, they didn't adopt native ways, but instead exploited them. During that period, fashionable men's hats were all the rage in Europe, and the hat-making industry required the raw material for felt—fur. The first choice was beaver, because the underfur was barbed and made strong felt.

Europe's beaver population had already been decimated, but the vastness of North America supported beavers in numbers beyond imagination, as well as a wealth of other furbearing animals. The Northwest Company and its competitors established posts throughout the hinterlands, where Indians could trade furs for muskets, iron cooking utensils, beads, and other items. Beaver pelts became backwoods currency.

Getting the furs from the continent's interior to the company headquarters in Montreal wasn't easy. Traders traveling by canoe couldn't complete the round trip during the open-water season. Grand Portage made a strategically located and accessible midway point. In the spring, canoes laden with furs left the remote trading posts, and others loaded with trade goods left Montreal. In mid-July they would rendezvous at Grand Portage, exchange their loads, and throw a bang up of a party. Two weeks later the brigades began their return trip.

The rendezvous had two sides. Outside the stockade French voyageurs, métis (people of mixed racial blood), and Indians—the Northwest Company's labor force—drank rum by the kegful. Inside, the company partners, who had traveled from Montreal, held business meetings in the great hall.

Of course, the Scotsmen who headed the Northwest Company (at one time fifty-two clans were represented) knew nothing of wildlife management or sustainable yield. Each year, as the industrious rodents were exterminated, trappers had to venture farther to find beaver. The change in North Woods topography that occurred when beaver disappeared must have been astonishing. Intricate networks of reservoirs and waterways, no doubt far larger than present-day beaver ponds, ran dry when the beaver were no longer there to maintain them. This was the first step in the mass destruction of North American wetlands that still continues.

The Scotsmen were loyalists, and Grand Portage was located on the rebels' side of the Pigeon River. Not only that, but the upstart United States was considering taxing goods that came across the portage. In 1800, the company began relocating the post to the Kaministiqua River, and in 1803 the first rendezvous was held at the new Fort William. In 1804, the smaller XY Company, which had also operated at Grand Portage, merged with the Northwest Company and became part of the Fort William operation. In 1822 when surveyor David Thompson returned to the post at Grand Portage he found only a field of clover. The portage was blocked by windfalls. The fur trade dwindled during the 1820s as mountain men penetrated the American Rockies and Europe became enamored of silk from the Far East. During the 1830s John Jacob Astor's American Fur Company had a fishing operation at Grand Portage for a short time, but the only continuous residents have been the Indian people, who lived there before the Europeans arrived and remain there still.

During the 1930s the Grand Portage Reservation began archeological and restoration work at the site with the assistance of the Minnesota Historical Society. By 1939 a stockade and great hall had been constructed on the original foundations. World War II brought a halt to the work. The National Park Service became involved with the project during the 1950s, and the Grand Portage Band provided 709 acres of land to the federal government for the establishment of the national monument.

The first stockade and great hall stood into the 1960s, but the great hall burned in 1969. Now on the site you will find a great hall, kitchen, and warehouse that were completed in the 1970s. All stand on their original locations. Plans are on the drawing board for a new visitor's center, but Congress has yet to appropriate the money to build it.

Visitors find the staff dressed in period costumes. The monument displays artifacts from archeological digs at the site, although most of the twenty thousand items that have been recovered are housed with the Minnesota Historical Society in St. Paul. Also on display are various furs and other items from the fur trade, including a fur press similar to the ones used to compress beaver pelts into ninety-pound bales. Gardeners will be intrigued by the small plot just a stone's throw from the lake.

On the shoreline in front of the stockade a dock extends into the bay. The *Wenonah,* which makes daily trips to Isle Royale, departs from here.

Hiking the Grand Portage

Hikers who wish to cross the historic portage have several options, all of which involve plenty of exercise. The first option is to begin the route at the stockade, walk to Fort Charlotte, and then return, a round trip of eighteen miles. Get an early start and plan to be on the trail all day. You'll want to carry food and water along.

The second option, and the one that most hikers choose, is to drive inland on County Road 17 to where the portage crosses "the old highway." You can park there and then hike in about five miles to Fort Charlotte. This is still a fair stroll, but it should allow you enough time to dally along the trail and to take the one-mile spur trail to the cascades of the Pigeon. Here the river makes a nearly 180-degree bend in a deep gorge and drops over a series of waterfalls. Portions of a flume built by the Pigeon River Lumber Company to carry logs through the area are still visible.

The third option requires a truck, a compass, and a nonhiker. You can have someone drive you along the rough road to Partridge Falls on the Pigeon upstream of Fort Charlotte. From there you can make your way on footpaths, overgrown logging roads, and moose trails to Fort Charlotte. Some say this hike takes forty-five minutes, but don't be alarmed if you spend two hours thrashing through the brush. This route is for the adventuresome only.

Is any hike to Fort Charlotte worth the effort? That depends on what you plan to find. Although two centuries ago the stockade and post there were as large as the Grand Portage facility, nothing remains. A tiny cleared area along the riverbank gives you a place to rest and includes a couple of primitive campsites. Be forewarned that this is prime mosquito habitat.

Archeologists have determined that the landing used by the voyageurs was a short distance upstream. The present trail, though, closely follows the historic route. The Park Service has added some welcome improvements, such as planks in the muddiest areas (wear boots!) and a boardwalk across an active beaver pond. The heavily wooded trail offers no views or vistas other than the cascades. This forest, like most of the North Shore, isn't "virgin," but has burned and been logged since the fur-trade era.

Before complaining about the bugs, the mud, the rocks, the heat, or the distance, modern portagers should consider this. Voyageurs crossing the portage regularly carried two ninety-pound packs, although they were paid extra if they carried more. They traveled at a dogtrot, taking advantage of the *poses* or rest stops, located about every half mile. The voyageurs completed a one-way trip in three to four hours. That's enough to give pause to even an ultra-marathoner.

Those with neither the time nor endurance to cross the Grand Portage can climb Mount Rose, which looms above the stockade. A short trail climbs three hundred feet to the hill's summit. From there you can look down on the stockade and Grand Portage Bay.

Isle Royale

Those who know it call it simply The Island. You needn't say more, although the name Isle Royale certainly shows the esteem explorers had for this beautiful place. No doubt, earlier adventurers—Indians who traveled offshore in frail canoes to mine copper and catch fish—had a similar reverence for this special island. Today it is a national park, an honor bestowed upon our most precious national treasures.

Isle Royale, managed as a wilderness, has no roads, and only nonmotorized travel is allowed. A 166-mile network of backpacking trails leads to thirty-six primitive camping areas. Rock Harbor Lodge, operated by National Park Concessions, is the only place where you can sleep in a bed. Isle Royale National Park is open from mid-April through the end of October.

Two ferries, the *Wenonah* and the *Voyageur II*, travel to Isle Royale from Grand Portage. The *Wenonah* makes daily round trips to Windigo. The *Voyageur II* makes a two-day trip around the island, spending the night at Rock Harbor Lodge. It's possible to make a spur-of-the-moment trip to Isle Royale, but it pays to plan ahead.

What's out there? Some would say paradise. The vegetation and terrain resemble the North Shore's, but innumerable coves and harbors punctuate the shoreline. The island contains several inland lakes, and dozens of offshore islands are available for power boaters and sailors to explore.

Isle Royale's best-known residents are wolves and moose. The interactions of predator and prey have been monitored for two decades. In recent years the island wolf population has begun to decline. Two possible reasons are interbreeding and the introduction of canine parvovirus from domestic pets. Although dogs are not allowed on the island, wolves travel across the ice from the mainland.

MILEPOST
146

If you turn around at Grand Portage, you'll miss the most spectacular scenery along the North Shore. Highway 61 climbs several hundred feet to the top of Mount Josephine. Several waysides offer panoramic views. Mount Josephine is a diabase sill comprised of

Mount Josephine

rock that may be 1.3 billion years old, some of the oldest in the world. In rock cuts along the highway you can see softer slates that are eroding.

Josephine presented an obstacle to highway construction. This portion of the road was planned in 1922 but not completed until the early 1960s. Engineers once considered a tunnel, but eventually decided to go over the top. At the time of construction Mount Josephine was so remote that the contractor purchased two new 2 1/2-yard steam shovels for the job and erected them on the site. A total of one million yards of rock and dirt were excavated, including a black pastelike glacial drift material that was almost impossible to scrape or dump.

Recently construction crews tangled once again with the cantankerous mountain as they built the state rest area overlooking Grand Portage Bay. It is open from May through October. Inside you can get travel information about the North Shore and all of Minnesota. On a clear day you can see Isle Royale.

At the summit an unmarked pull-off on the north side of the highway overlooks Teal Lake. The lake lies at the bottom of a huge, rocky bowl. In autumn the yellows of birches splash the hillsides. During winter the black cliffs provide alpinelike contrast to the snowy landscape. If you scan the northern horizon, you'll see distant clear-cuts. These lie across the Pigeon River in Canada.

On the east side of Mount Josephine you can look out on Lake Superior from two waysides. In the shallows of Wauswaugoning Bay, Indians once speared fish by torchlight. If you look carefully, you may see the fluorescent orange floats that mark the nets of commercial fishermen. The archipelago lying off the bay is the Susie Islands, home to several species of rare subarctic plants. No one lives there now, although an early settler once fished there and operated a small copper mine.

The landform east of the Susies is Pigeon Point, the tip

of the Minnesota Arrowhead. Believe it or not, the Michigan border lies about a mile offshore from the point. Beyond the point you can see the waters of Pigeon Bay and the Ontario coast. In the distance lies Isle Royale. The flashing light off the southwestern end of the island comes from the Rock of Ages Lighthouse.

High Falls

MILEPOST 150 The Pigeon River, one of the largest rivers on the Minnesota coast, forms a lengthy border with Ontario. However, it isn't called the Pigeon until it leaves South Fowl Lake. Unlike most North Shore rivers, it isn't a trout stream. Instead the Pigeon supports warmer-water species, such as walleyes and northern pike

The Pigeon played an important role in history as one of the water highways of the fur-trade era. This watershed was also rich in timber. Loggers held pulpwood drives on the river until 1932. You can see the remains of an old logging sluiceway on the Canadian side of High Falls, which at 130 feet is Minnesota's highest waterfall.

For years the land along the river at High Falls was privately owned, and a roadside tourist operation once did business here. In the late 1980s the land became public property. The Grand Portage Band is working with the state to develop the site as a day-use state park. Construction is scheduled to begin in 1992, and the park will open by 1993. Planners say the emphasis is on simplicity—no campground, just a picnic area and trails to the overlook above the falls. A small visitor center at the highway entrance will house an office and restrooms.

Until the park is completed, officials would prefer that you not use the area. You can see the falls (and actually get a better view) from Middle Falls Provincial Park on the Canadian side. Thirty-foot Middle Falls is just a short distance upstream. You will be able to reach it from a hiking trail in the new High Falls State Park.

How's the fishing in the Pigeon? Not bad, although access is somewhat difficult. Walleyes and northerns make up most of the catch. You must have a Grand Portage Indian Reservation permit to fish the river.

Canada Customs

Citizen of what country? Last name, please. And how long will you be in Canada?

Most people feel intimidated by customs agents. The rapid-fire questions and the possibility of having their belongings searched makes people uneasy, even if they have nothing to hide. Often travelers are unsure of what they can and cannot bring across the border. The following summary of Canadian customs regulations should answer some common questions. However, regulations can change, and this book is not the final authority. If you have questions, contact a Canada customs office.

Identification

You must have proof of citizenship for each member of your party, including children. Birth certificates or passports are the best, although a drivers license should suffice. If you are traveling with a child other than your own, have a signed letter of permission from the child's parent or guardian. If you have a criminal record, contact Canadian immigrations officials prior to your trip.

Food, liquor, and tobacco

You are allowed to bring a two-day supply of food into Canada, but there are no hard-and-fast answers about what constitutes a two-day supply. You can bring items such as meat and fruit for personal use. Food destined for resale in Canada requires special permits.

A case of beer or forty ounces of spirits or wine per person is allowed. You can bring an additional gallon of spirits per person if you pay Canadian duty and tax, which isn't cheap. Any greater amount of alcohol requires special permission from the Liquor Control Board of Ontario. Another option is to purchase alcohol at a duty-free shop. You then avoid U.S. taxes, but still must pay Canadian tax.

Smokers can have two hundred cigarettes (one carton) or fifty cigars or two hundred grams of tobacco per person. However, if you are just going to Canada for the day, bring only the amount of cigarettes you plan to smoke. Customs officers won't allow day-trippers to bring in a carton.

Pets

Dogs over three months of age must have a certificate verifying that rabies vaccinations are up-to-date. You can get the certificate from your veterinarian. No certificates are needed for cats. Pets must be in good health; those with obvious ailments may not be allowed to cross the border.

Weapons

You cannot bring handguns into Canada. Also prohibited are Mace, stun guns, billy clubs, and switchblades. Hunters are allowed to bring rifles and shotguns. However, you won't be allowed to bring long guns into Canada when hunting seasons are not open. If you intend to do so, be sure to contact customs in advance. If customs officials find a prohibited weapon in your possession, you'll be arrested.

Gasoline

Unites States citizens receive no personal gasoline allotment. However, customs officials allow a ten-gallon "float." For example, you can bring a six-gallon can of gasoline for your outboard motor without paying tax or duties. If your gasoline supply exceeds ten gallons, you'll be required to pay duties and taxes on the entire amount. You don't have to pay duties or taxes on the gasoline in your vehicle.

Live bait

You cannot bring live minnows into Canada. Leeches, waxworms, and worms are allowed. However, worms must be packed in a processed bedding, not dirt.

Tips for easy crossings

The Canada customs station at Pigeon River is open continuously year-round. However, due to the current disparity between U.S. and Canadian prices, you'll often find long lines of returning Canadian shoppers at the border. Crossing early in the morning is the best way to avoid waiting in line. If you have goods that may require inspection by customs officials, make sure they are easy to reach. Organize the goods in groups of similar items.

Sales tax rebates

Many goods and services in Canada are subject to expensive sales taxes, both a federal tax called GST and a provincial tax called PST. United States citizens can receive tax rebates. Here's how.

Save all your sales receipts. When you return to the border, stop at the Canada customs station and pick up the necessary rebate forms. When you get home, mail completed forms and copies of your sales receipts to the addresses listed on the forms. You must mail in the forms—you cannot get the rebate at the customs station.

You have now completed your excursion along the beautiful, wild coast of Minnesota's North Shore. You may choose to continue your journey by following the 1300-mile Lake Superior Circle Route through Ontario, Upper Michigan, and Wisconsin.

However, if you turn around and head back down Highway 61 you'll see the North Shore from an entirely new perspective as you travel from east to west.

Continue Your Journey

Other fine books from  Pfeifer-Hamilton Publishers

CampSights
Sam Cook

Another delightful collection of essays and stories from the North Country. Sam offers insights into the subtleties of the natural world that all too often go unnoticed. Sam's first two books, *Up North* and *Quiet Magic*, are also available from Pfeifer-Hamilton Publishers.

Hardcover, 208 pages, $16.95

Teaching Kids to Love the Earth
Marina L. Herman, Ann Schimpf, Joseph Passineau, and Paul Treuer

A collection of 186 earth-caring activities designed for use with children of all ages to help them experience and appreciate the Earth. *Teaching Kids to Love the Earth* will enable you and the children you work with to experience a sense of wonder about the world we all share.

Softcover, 192 pages, $14.95

Canoe Country Camping: Wilderness Skills for the Boundary Waters and Quetico
Michael Furtman

Entertaining, up-to-date, and complete, *Canoe Country Camping* has everything you'll need to enjoy a safe and fun-filled camping trip. You will find detailed drawings, helpful charts, and handy checklists. *Canoe Country Camping* is a great gift for seasoned canoeists as well as beginners.

Softcover, 216 pages, $14.95

Canoe Country Wildlife:
A Field Guide to the Boundary Waters and Quetico
Mark Stensaas

Written for the "curious naturalist" in each of us, *Canoe Country Wildlife* introduces you to the wildlife you are most likely to see as you travel in the North Woods. Filled with fascinating facts, handy checklists, and suggested activities, it is a wonderful gift for anyone who enjoys the outdoors.

Softcover, 240 pages, $14.95

Gunflint: Reflections on the Trail
Justine Kerfoot

Justine Kerfoot has lived on Minnesota's remote Gunflint Trail for five decades. She's gutsy and knowledgeable and humorous, most of all she's real—a unique woman of strength and character! Her keen observations and warm sensitivity recreate memorable episodes and touching moments from her years on the trail.

Softcover, 208 pages, $12.95

Distant Fires
Scott Anderson

A classic canoe-trip story, with a twist of wry. Anderson's journey began on a front porch in Duluth, Minnesota, and ended three months and 1,700 miles later at historic York Factory in Hudson Bay. The reader is treated to a breath of fresh northwoods air with every turn of the page.

Softcover, 176 pages, $12.95

To order, write or call:

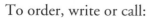

Pfeifer-Hamilton Publishers
210 West Michigan
Duluth MN 55802-1908

Toll Free   800-247-6789
Fax   218-727-0505
Local   218-727-0500